REVIVING INDUSTRY IN AMERICA

Ballinger Series in

BUSINESS IN A GLOBAL ENVIRONMENT

S. Prakash Sethi, Series Editor

Center for Management
Baruch College
The City University of New York

REVIVING INDUSTRY IN AMERICA
Japanese Influences on Manufacturing and the Service Sector

HARRIS JACK SHAPIRO
TERESA COSENZA

BALLINGER PUBLISHING COMPANY
Cambridge, Massachusetts
A Subsidiary of Harper & Row, Publishers, Inc.

International Standard Book Number: 0-88730-118-5

Library of Congress Catalog Card Number: 87-17585

Printed in the United States of America

Library of Congress Cataloging-in-Publication Data

Shapiro, H. Jack (Harris Jack)
  Reviving industry in America.

  (Ballinger series in business in a global environment)
  Includes bibliographies and index.
  1. United States—Manufacturers—Management. 2. Service
industries—United States—Management. 3. Industrial management—
United States. 4. Japan—Manufactures—Management. 5. Service
industries—Japan—Management. 6. Industrial management—Japan.
I. Cosenza, Teresa. II. Title. III. Series.
HD9725.S46   1987   338.4'767'0973   87-17585
ISBN 0-88730-118-5

CONTENTS

LIST OF FIGURES

PREFACE

Much is known about the Japanese system of management, and much has been theorized about the possibility of transferring this system to other industrial environments (in particular, to the United States), but little has actually been done to prove or disprove the potential success of such a transplantation into a large base of American companies. We, the authors, do not believe that the final word on the matter will ever be reached, but what we present here represents a sizable cross-section of the major efforts that leading American manufacturers have made to increase productivity by borrowing from the Japanese. We queried over nine hundred companies, including the Fortune 500 and others, as well as Japanese companies operating in the United States, about their levels of success in implementing systems typically characterized as Japanese, such as just-in-time manufacturing, specialized quality control processes, management by teamwork, and widespread employee involvement in decisionmaking. With the letter, we supplied a list of techniques and methods commonly used in Japan. Many responded, often with invitations to visit so that interviews could be conducted in person. Our original letter and enclosure, along with some typical responses, are reproduced in the Appendix. To the many donors of this information, we express our sincerest gratitude for helping make our book as true a representation of the Americanization of Japanese management as could be made.

Much of what we have written has been based on many of the corporate publications we received. We would like to acknowledge the following companies for providing us with reference materials: Pitney Bowes, Champion Spark Plug, Omark Industries, AT&T, Whirlpool, General Dynamics, AMP Incorporated, Mitsui, Sheller-Globe, Enplas (U.S.A.), Honda of America, TRW, General Motors, GAF Corporation, Worthington Industries, Hershey Foods, General Electric, Outboard Marine, Monsanto, Boise Cascade, GTE Service Corporation, Springs Industries, Ford Motor Company, American Can Company, Richardson-Vicks, Nissan Motor Corporation, 3M, Xerox, Florida Power and Light, Atlantic Richfield, LTV Steel, USG Corporation, Mohasco Corporation, McGraw-Hill, Oak Industries, Owens-Corning, and the Ontario Paper Company. To all of these organizations, we extend our most heartfelt thanks.

JAPANESE AND AMERICAN INDUSTRIAL SYSTEMS

1 THE JAPANESE INDUSTRIAL MODEL

The key ingredient in the Japanese industrial model is Nenko—a system of cohesiveness and coordination developed by large Japanese companies. With a philosophy of pragmatism and a social structure of tightly organized clans, the birth of Nenko was almost inevitable. In this system, workers join a major corporation after graduation from junior high school, high school, or university, receive a great deal of in-company training and indoctrination, remain employed by the same organization for their entire work lives, and usually retire at age fifty-five to sixty. Employment is guaranteed, unless the firm is in such bad economic circumstances that it is in danger of going bankrupt. Business slowdowns and recessions are not grounds for dismissal. The permanence of the Nenko work force is further assured by the unwillingness of employers to hire anyone at a hierarchical level equivalent to the one he left at a previous firm. In fact, an employee from another company looking for a new job will only be hired, if at all, at the bottom of the promotion ladder. This lifetime employment leads to intense feelings of security and loyalty.

Part of the Nenko system is a seniority-based promotion arrangement. Everyone in a group hired at the same time is equal, and they all move through the promotion hierarchy as a group until the executive level is reached. A new hiree will go into a training-based job for three to five years. He will then routinely be promoted to a higher position where his training will continue. Then at least eight years must elapse after entering a company before a worker can hope to be promoted to the rank of sub-section chief.[1] After acquiring this rank, approximately fifteen years must elapse before he can achieve the rank of chief or "kacho" of a section. A deputy departmental position requires fifteen to twenty years of service. At least twenty years of service are required before one can hope to attain the rank of department manager or "bucho." Top management positions only open up for employees who are in their early fifties. Because members of a group do not know who will be chosen for the top managerial jobs for most of their working lives, there is great incentive to work harder and longer in order to be considered executive material. Poor workers are not discriminated against, but rather given every opportunity to improve their performance. Executives are eventually chosen according to the contributions they have made to the firm since beginning their careers. When selected, they serve a comparatively short time due to the mandatory retirement age of fifty-five to sixty.

All employees, from the individual who operates a basic machine to the company president, believe they are part of a family—a family that concerns itself not only with their lifetime employment, but also with other needs, such as housing, vacations, insurance, income-tax filing, and even matchmaking. The company president is the head of the surrogate family. The strong loyalties thus created are evidenced in intense competition between firms working in the same industry and between groups of workers performing similar tasks within a division. However, since there is no likelihood of being caught in survival and promotion struggles with other members of the company, competition is untainted by fear. Within the individual groups, cooperation is rife, and members protect each other against any unforeseen adversities. The interests of company employees, regardless of rank, are paramount, and only after the needs of labor and management people are met are the stockholders considered. The end result is a corporate society capable of fulfilling individual physiological and psychological needs.

Because current results are not prerequisites for continued employment, top management is free to engage in long-term strategic planning, even at the sacrifice of short-term profits. Long-term generalist job training is also possible because of lifetime employment practices. The key to generalist training is job rotation, which allows employees to acquire skills in many different specializations and develop a sense of how the various functions of an organization fit together. Job rotation is also a powerful socializing and internal-communication tool that helps eliminate "turf" problems, so common in American firms.

Obviously, it is very expensive to train an employee as a generalist; the training can take several years. However, if a person remains with a firm until his retirement, the cost of training can be amortized over thirty to thirty-five years, making it a minor corporate expense. In many American companies where career changes, job changes, and lay-offs are the norm rather than the exception, the cost to train an individual as a generalist can be prohibitive.

Generalist training is concomitant with decisionmaking by consensus, typical of the Japanese model. The Takeuchi article in Thurow's *The Management Challenge* explains the reasoning behind this process.

> Even a person holding a high position will not make a decision independently. First, he must order his subordinates or organization to study a matter and consider the conclusion reached before he makes a decision. If the president makes decisions by himself all the time on his own authority, he will soon lose the support of his subordinates and become unable to exercise his ability. His subordinates will feel hurt, turn their backs on him, and, in effect, ignore his orders, although they may pretend to obey them.

It may take a long time for the Japanese to reach consensus, but once made, a decision can be implemented rather quickly—everyone is familiar with the question, has provided their input, and has already agreed.

THE DEVELOPMENT OF THE NENKO SYSTEM

Japan's pluralistic culture blends components from many of its neighbors: Buddhism from India, the writing and reading format of ideographs from China, art appreciation and development from both Korea and China. This pluralism, according to Yamaazaki, led to a uniquely Japanese philosophy that he describes as "agnosticism without nihilism," a form of pragmatism or rationalism based upon the process of trial and error, and on the willingness to study objective facts in order to understand the relationship between those facts.[3]

Burma claims that the Nenko system is the offspring of this social structure.[4] Age-old rituals and ceremonies, scrupulously observed by many firms in diverse industries, underpin the system. Toward the end of the Edo period (the late nineteenth century), Japan, with its established philosophical and social structures, began to show an interest in almost everything Western—art, history, language, culture, and business. This attention to Western business prompted an interest in how it was being managed.

A complementary school of thought believes that although the conditions for a Nenko-type system existed, it did not become part of Japanese industrial life until after World War I. At that time the Japanese experienced a large industrial boom resulting in the need for a large, stable labor force. Sumiya cites the example of a shipyard owned by Mitsubishi-Nagaski in the 1920s.[5] The attrition rate then was 52 percent. Obviously, it was impossible to maintain a working organization with more than half of the yard's blue-collar workers continually leaving. To overcome this critical, probably fatal condition, top management instituted several drastic measures. First, they recruited only from farms and educational institutions. Then, they trained the recruits to give them specialized skills, adaptable only to their own company and industry, that is, generalist training within a specialized industry.

The methods begun after World War I were further refined and developed after World War II. Under the shadow of an American occupation force and intensive labor unrest, the Zaibatsu, the corporate giants that dominated pre-war Japan, strictly began to enforce seniority promotions and lifetime employment practices. As a result of company policy and vertical unionization, employees were no longer discharged because of poor economic conditions. To further stabilize the employment situation, they developed a procedure where wages were highly correlated to length of service. This "holding tool" is still common practice in Nenko-type firms. Employees are usually underpaid for approximately the first half of their work lives. To recoup this significant investment, they must remain with their companies, where they will be overpaid during the latter half of their careers. This practice is actually a form of deferred compensation and is very effective in preventing outbreaks of job-hopping.

The end of the war brought about another fundamental modification of Japanese business practices. Quality control techniques were imported from the United States through the offices of statistician W. Edwards Deming so that the restored Japanese industries could start afresh with new systems geared to the production of quality goods.

ELEMENTS OF THE NENKO SYSTEM

Staffing

If large Japanese manufacturing organizations did not place constraints on Nenko, total wage requirements would go out of control. With no dismissals and wage levels reflective of length of service, a firm's payroll would be forever increasing. To prevent this, the number of entering employees is strictly limited, based on the organization being minimally staffed. Temporary, subcontract, daily, and retired workers are used to flesh out the permanent skeletons of Nenko organizations.

This practice has given rise to a dual-wage and dual-labor market in Japan. In medium-small firms, wages are approximately 80 percent of those paid in the large companies. Even more drastic is the difference in wages paid by firms employing one to three people. Only about one-third of the entire Japanese labor pool is actually engaged in Nenko-practicing companies, a number that has not increased significantly over the past ten to fifteen years. In addition, benefits, such as pensions, housing facilities, vacations, loans, and the like, are seldom provided to employees outside the Nenko system. Medium-small companies do not guarantee employment, and an inordinately large number of these firms fail. Because of this, job satisfaction in medium-small companies is relatively low and may indeed be partly responsible for the reported high accident rates, six times higher in firms that employ 30 to 99 people than that in companies with over 1000 people. To worsen matters, most of these companies do not cover their workers with health and hospital insurance.

Unions

Japanese unions play a role quite different from that of their American counterparts. Most large Japanese companies are unionized, while the smaller ones are not. The unions are enterprise-wide, vertically arranged, and include most employees, white-collar as well as blue-collar, up to the rank of Assistant Section Manager. They usually include all divisions, groups, and sections, and cross industry lines. Being, in effect, "company unions," they act in concert with the firm to protect the older workers' pay and benefits. Workers at the foreman level usually have leadership roles in the unions. These people, who have put in many years of underpaid service in lower-ranked jobs, now find themselves in a position to enjoy some of the fruits of their past labors. They are not about to rock the corporate boat, especially since they could return to their regular jobs when their union leadership terms end. They may also end up being in top management later on in their work lives. Japanese union members know that their welfare depends directly on how successful their companies are and therefore strongly support the concepts of improved efficiency and effectiveness that lead to greater productivity.

Overtime and Vacations

Overtime, usually not compensated, is the rule rather than the exception. Whether brought on by group pressure, individual motivation, or both, overtime is increasing. Neff reports that average monthly overtime per manufacturing employee has grown to 21.1 hours in 1982 from 13.8 hours in 1960. He also states that in a Hitachi Ltd. plant in Yokohama the union agreed-upon amount of obligatory overtime is forty hours per month per worker.[6] However, many employees put in much more than is required by contract.

The same applies to vacations. The average employee is entitled to four weeks of vacation a year; however, only some of the clerical and blue-collar people take advantage of this. Managers seldom take anywhere near the full holiday time allotted to them. Vacations of less than one week a year are common for fear of being considered non-company-oriented and harming one's work group. The company's image and its welfare are always paramount to the worker.

Male Domination

Throughout this chapter, the authors have referred to employees or workers as "he." It is deliberate. Women play an insignificant role in

Japanese industrial life, although the overall picture is changing slightly. At the present time, approximately 1 percent of all managers in Japan are women. This is not because there is a shortage of college-educated women—in fact thousands graduate from the universities each year. But they are not trained to be managers because they usually leave their firms after marriage and most certainly after having a child. There is thus no motivation to train women as generalists—training absolutely required to become a manager. To compound the situation even further, the law limits the amount of overtime a woman can work. It is far less than is normally expected and received from a man.

In this male-dominated industrial society, night clubs are frequented several nights a week by male managers for the purpose of drinking and socializing with their peers, a fraternization very important in developing a corporate group dynamic. Women employees are not welcome at these occasions, and so they are barred from entrance into the corporate inner circles.

CRITICISMS

The Japanese approach to modern industrialization is not without its shortcomings. They have been described by several critics. In a journal article,[7] Sherman introduces Kamata's book, *Japan in the Passing Lane*, particularly his attempt to explain what it means to be a seasonal (nonpermanent) worker at Toyota, where he worked for a six-month period on the assembly line.[8] Kamata chose to work for Toyota because he heard it had the poorest working conditions of any automobile plant in Japan. He claims that the game plan at all Japanese automobile factories is to produce more and more with fewer and fewer workers. Productivity increases are credited to speeding up the assembly line and mandating excessive overtime and holiday work. Assembly-line workers perceive themselves as machines, not people. Sherman, trying to verify the accusations of brutal and callous treatment of nonpermanent workers at Toyota and Honda, as evidenced by Kamata's personal experience and hearsay, interviewed a half-dozen Japanese managers and executives from three different organizations, all of whom denied Kamata's claims. One independent businessman not affiliated to a major corporation stated that Kamata's findings were "journalistic sensationalism," not an accurate portrayal of Japanese factory life. Sherman also states that these views were confirmed by the 383 American employees of the Nissan plant in Smyrna, Tennessee, who were sent to Japan to observe the parent company in operation before the start-up of their unit in the United States. Even so, Sherman still feels that there are a few serpents here and there in the Japanese workman's Garden of Eden. A much stronger negative approach is taken by Kotkin and Kishimoto who feel that fear, which they term "Theory F," is the driving force behind the Japanese industrial system. They believe most senior management people would like to leave their present companies and join other firms but are unable to do so because of the way their personal needs are intertwined with those of the company. They quote one top manager: "The problem is there is nowhere to go. You soon realize that your car, your vacations, your expense account, your pension all belong to the company. The way the system works, without the company, the big company, you are nothing." Makiyo Mizobuchi, executive director of Recruit Jinzai Center Co., one of Japan's leading job-placement agencies is quoted as saying, "Executives in the big companies tend to forget the rest of the world exists. He sees the company as everything. He ignores reality and just works. He forgets his family, loses his identity in the corporation."[9]

There are innumerable horror stories in the literature of Japanese managers who for some reason or another were passed over for promotion. At the top of the hierarchy there is only room for a few; a mistake in judgment or the inability to produce can lead to, as Mizobuchi calls it, a "trail of suffering." Those left behind no longer have any duties to speak of and sit at their desks looking out the window or reading their newspapers, waiting until they turn fifty-five so they can officially retire. It is a strange form of working retirement. Sometimes when a manager at the section level is passed over for promotion, he is transferred to one of the company's smaller divisions or affiliates. To save face, the transfer may be presented to the manager as a promotion, although, it signals in reality a definitive loss of prestige and power. Despite the pain and grief caused by the transfer, the individual is expected to exhibit enthusiasm, concealing without complaint his troubles. In Japanese he is displaying "gaman," and he has little choice but to do so. Probably no other comparable company would hire him, and even if one did, he would have a terribly difficult time working with his new subordinates since he would be considered an outsider, or even worse, a "gajjin," or foreigner.

As a result of work-related stresses such as twelve-hour days, six-day weeks, and little to no vacation time, there has been an increase in the Japanese suicide rate and problems with alcoholism. *Business Week*[10] reports that suicides in Tokyo among males aged thirty-five to fifty-nine have more than doubled, increasing from 4,429 in 1975 to 10,128 in 1984, though the population increased by a mere 8 percent. They also state that work-related stress has caused a sharp rise in the number of men who have left their families and companies to begin new lives under aliases. Alcohol is estimated to be a problem for 3 percent of the male population. Although significant, it is still only about a third of the American male alcoholic rate of 9 percent. To counteract the debilitating effects of work stress, men in their forties and fifties are beginning—often at their own expense—to seek psychological and psychiatric help at mental clinics—a practice that was unheard of previously.

CONCLUSION

Weighing as fairly as possible all the pros and cons, one can conclude that the Nenko-based Japanese paradigm, with all its faults, is the most highly developed, sophisticated, and successful industrial model in the world. The cohesiveness generated by the surrogate family concept allows the large Japanese firm to operate very effectively within the rigid Nenko structure without shattering it. The system provides security to its employees while demanding loyalty within an internal environment that provides very little breathing space. Peer pressure to conform to group standards is the acceptable norm. To an outsider, to be an average worker in a large Japanese company would probably be a fate worse than death. But Japanese society is not designed to cater to individuals. Expressions of individualism in the work place are viewed as manifestations of immaturity, while a definitive sign of maturity is the ability to be integrated into a group and work for the common good of the group and the organization of which it is a part.

Nenko has helped develop Japanese companies into paternalistic, highly efficient, mechanistic structures. Workers are treated with respect and are made to feel important at all levels within the organization. They know they are important to the welfare of the company, and the company reciprocates by being deeply concerned about their welfare. The system is uniquely Japanese, geared to the needs and wants of the people within it.

In addition, the current model has also been substantially influenced by the Japanese government. There really is a "Japan Incorporated," which is represented by the powerful Ministry of International Trade and Industry (MITI). Along with the Japanese banks, MITI has played a major role in the reindustrialization of Japan and its resulting prosperity. The model has also been greatly influenced by American quality control techniques introduced into Japanese industry after World War II. That the model not only works but works very well is obvious when one assesses the industrial miracle of post–World War II Japan.

NOTES

1. M. Y. Yoshio, *Japan's Management System: Tradition and Innovation* (Cambridge, Mass.: MIT Press, 1968), 229–30.

2. Hiroshi Takeuchi, "Motivation and Productivity," in *The Management Challenge: Japanese Views*, ed. Lester C. Thurow (Cambridge, Mass.: MIT Press, 1985), 26.

3. Masakazu Yamaazaki, "The Impact of Japanese Culture on Management," in *The Management Challenge: Japanese Views*, ed. Lester C. Thurow, 31–41 (Cambridge, Mass.: MIT Press, 1985).

4. I. Burma, "Company on the Job in Japan," *Pam Am Clipper*, September 1981.

5. M. Sumiya, *Social Impact of Industrialization in Japan* (Tokyo: Japanese Commission for UNESCO, 1963).

6. Robert Neff, "The Other Side of the Japanese Miracle," *International Management* (October 1982): 19–20.

7. George Sherman, "Japanese Management: Separating Fact from Fiction," *National Productivity Review* (Winter 1984–85): 75–77.

8. S. Kamata, *Japan in the Passing Lane* (New York: Pantheon Books, 1982).

9. Joel Kotkin and Yoriko Kishimoto, "Theory F," *Inc.*, April 1986, 55.

10. Leslie Helm and Charles Gaffney, "The High Price Japanese Pay for Success," *Business Week*, April 7, 1986, 52–54.

2 THE AMERICAN INDUSTRIAL MODEL

The American industrial model has no key concept such as the Nenko system behind it. Many of the specifics and non-specifics adopted into our system have roots that go back thousands of years and are traceable to many different civilizations. But it is safe to say that the Industrial Revolution marked the true beginning of the modern model.

This period, from 1700 to about 1785, saw the birth of the factory system and its emphasis on production, quality, and financial controls. The concept of planning began to take hold. Adam Smith proclaimed the advantages of the division of labor and the power of the market place. Movement was made toward scientific management, while technology provided the means for large-scale interchangeable parts manufacturing.

In the first half of the nineteenth century, manufacturing began to replace foreign trade as America's major industry. In 1813, modern, large-scale, integrated corporate manufacturing came of age and spread rapidly, beginning with the Waltham system of steel manufacturing. Agriculture followed, becoming the country's primary business endeavor in the latter half of the nineteenth century. The country became trade and market oriented, as well as job specialized. The system was distorted, however, by the use of slave labor. The Civil War and its aftermaths, along with the opening of the West, moved the economic base away from agriculture. The system was now fueled by regional trade and manufacturing, demanding improved and diversified transportation methods. Railroads began to span the country, facilitating the movement of labor, raw materials, and finished goods that further accelerated the American industrial revolution.

No discussion of the development of the American industrial model would be complete without a mention of the Protestant Work Ethic—our legacy from the Protestant Reformation and John Calvin.

Calvinism stripped its followers of the shelter of a forgiving church and thrust them naked under the eye of God, demanding they so discipline their faith, time, and work that they could withstand scrutiny. The Pilgrim fathers, austere in dress and demeanor, were encouraged by their faith to work hard to gain material wealth and social status. Worldly success and prosperity were signs of God's grace and possible salvation for the elect.

Without the example of a leisured, European-styled autocracy, and with labor in short supply, the grandchildren of the Puritans pushed their way into occupations in which they could be their own masters, with room for independence and innovation.[1] Individualism flourished, as it still does in today's highly competitive business climate. Capitalism thus took root early on in our history, and its hold remained firm during the nineteenth century despite the devastating effects of the Civil War and severe economic depressions.

TAYLORISM

At the beginning of the twentieth century, the United States led the world into the era of industrial giants. Between 1898 and 1903, tremendous waves of consolidation and centralization took place. The concept of "bigness" had, and continues to have, enormous appeal. The monopolization of an industry allowed owner-management to directly control supply and demand, hence price and profit. United States Steel Corporation and Standard Oil Company of New Jersey were formed. One thousand and forty separate railroad lines were consolidated into six huge combinations controlling almost $10 billion (in 1900 dollars) of capital. Management realized it needed new organizational techniques and structures to control and operate these vast, newly formed industrial groupings with their thousands of employees.

In 1911, Frederick W. Taylor published *The Principles of Scientific Management*, his attempt to bring time-honored work methods into the realm of scientific endeavor by understanding the rationale and logic behind them. His research involved gathering data regarding workmen's practices, scientifically analyzing it, systemizing his findings, and developing and applying his derived "scientific management" rules, laws, and formulas. According to Taylor, management's responsibility was to " . . . scientifically select and train, teach and develop the workman . . . and . . . heartily cooperate with the men so as to insure all of the work was being done in accordance with the principles."[2]

In Taylor's view, a major problem in American industry was the unwillingness of workers to perform to their potential; the labor class was deliberately attempting to work against management by controlling their own productivity. He believed it was possible to determine individual productivity levels and establish requirements by objective analyses of data collected in the workplace. Reactions against Taylorism were strong. Labor unions, humanitarian organizations, and some members of the government accused him of treating people as machines. In effect, the charges were true: his methodology held job requirements to be the constraints to which worker inputs had to conform. In other words, the job determined the worker, who either matched its requirements or was replaced.

Controversy swirled about Taylor in his lifetime, and seventy-five years later his ideas are still cause for disagreement among today's practitioners and academics. As an example of these differing points of view, Edwards argues that it is wrong to look at Taylorism as a management practice, because it was never really implemented.[3] He believes the system was too complicated, and employees became impactient long before its final elements could be installed and the concepts tested in the workplace. Juravich believes that one of the reasons Taylorism has not been more widely accepted in the American workplace is that scientific management was derived from worker's knowledge, and managers and engineers did not and do not attribute much usable knowledge to the average workman or laborer, whom they consider essentially unintelligent and unskilled.[4] There are, however, those who strongly believe that the effects of Taylor's work are still felt in the business world of today. Regardless of the arguments, the fact is that Taylor's rules, regulations, and concepts, although modified by time, have provided our present industrial model with some of its most important building blocks. Many American organizations are run according to the notion that the functions of workers and managers must always be strictly distinct. Obviously, this is a major point of divergence between American and Japanese management practices.

BUREAUCRACY

Around 1910, Max Weber's ideas of bureaucracy began to permeate the American industrial scene. With the formation of megacorporations in the early 1900s, capitalism needed a new and/or modified structural arrangement, and bureaucracy became the dominant format. The concept was not new. It had existed for centuries in such organizations as the Catholic Church, the Roman Army, and the Arsenal of Venice. Built on hierarchy, written rules and regulations, specialized training, specified fields of competence, separation of ownership and administration, legal authority, and absence of appropriation of official positions by incumbents, it is a pure form of impersonal organization. Merton described bureaucracy as a system based on strict formality between workers and a strongly enforced social hierarchy among persons occupying different positions within a private- or public-sector group.[5] In theory, all personalized relationships are eliminated, and nonrational behavior is not tolerated by the organization. The bureaucratic model is deliberately mechanistic. Employee inputs are strictly based on organization requirements. If it were possible, human beings would be excluded from the organization, since bureaucratic reasoning attributes most problems to human foibles.

Weber's bureaucratic model is rigidly structured and would undoubtably fracture in normal practice unless modified. The forms of such a bureaucracy become ends instead of means to many supervisors, leading to a status-quo structural arrangement, blind conformance, resistance to technological innovation, and minimal organization performance. In addition, researchers such as Williams, Sjoberg, and Sjoberg believe that the very nature of bureaucracy tends to foster hidden and undesirable arrangements within an organization. Referencing Thompson,[6] they state:

> If managers are to sustain rationality, they must delegate considerable responsibility to subordinates to perform the more mundane chores of bureau-

cracy. Yet the delegation of responsibility, particularly to individuals who command highly specialized skills and technical knowledge, tends to undermine the hierarchical arrangements, including the positions of the immediate supervisors of these specialists.

To avoid erosion of their power and authority, managers create their own hidden world. They protect themselves by delegating "blamability" under the guise of responsibility, for the responsibility accorded underlings incurs more potential for blame than for rights and privileges.[7]

Henri Fayol redefined the concept of bureaucratic management in fourteen principles based upon his experience as an executive in France's mining industry. His contributions to the field of management earned him the sobriquet, "father of functional management."[8] He supplied some of the elasticity necessary for industrial bureaucracy to work, through concepts such as functional division of work, authority, discipline, control, unity of command, centralization, scalar chain, and equity, among others.

Company Unions

To alleviate some of the problems associated with a strict bureaucracy and its associated labor problems (such as those generated by "blamability"), company unions began to form with the blessing of management. The firms involved began to realize, especially after World War I, that there was a definite need to improve their working relations with their blue-collar employees as well as some of their white-collar managers and professionals. The company union was an especially useful tool, since it gave workers a chance to vent their feelings, while allowing management to maintain control of the work force and, in effect, freeze out organized labor's attempts to unionize their plants. In vogue from about 1910 to the end of the thirties, these company unions, also known as "Employee Representation Plans," were bitterly opposed by organized labor. Finally, as a result of various law suits instituted by organized labor, the United States Supreme Court ruled in 1938 that company unions violated the National Labor Relations Act because they were dominated by management.

The company-union arrangements did serve some purpose in easing employer-employee relationships. Most of them had shop committees composed of both labor and management. Formal meetings gave labor committee members a chance to express their concerns about working conditions, work methods, compensation, grievances, and time-and-motion standards. Still, in most of the cases where agreement could not be reached in the committee, upper-level management resolved disputes using the rationale, "be reasonable—do it my way." In rare instances were disputes settled by impartial arbitrators.

MODEL FORMATION

The combination of Taylor's scientific management and the Weber-Fayol model as moderated by company unionism gave rise to a school we term "classical management." This classical, or mechanistic, school of management was later modified by the human-relations movement (organistic management) during the 1920s through the thirties and forties. It began with the Elton Mayo studies at Western Electric, which arrived at the amazing conclusion that people like to be treated as human beings, not as appendages to machines. Human-relation concepts such as closed-shop unionism and fringe benefits helped divert the potential labor problems caused by World War II, which limited labor mobility in the labor-short market and mandated the freezing of wages. The 1950s and 1960s ushered in the neoclassical school, marked by such concepts as profit centers—decentralized, multidivision companies with coordinated, centralized corporate control, as typified by Alfred P. Sloan's structuring of General Motors and Pierre du Pont's structuring of Du Pont. The latest input to our industrial model is modern behavioral science and its by-products, organizational behavior discipline, which got its start in American universities and colleges in the late 1950s and early 1960s and is still being taught today as a major specialization in our MBA and doctoral programs in business. Modern study of organizational behavior is grounded in a strict scientific methodology and delves into the related areas of motivation, satisfaction, compensation, leadership, structure, and group dynamics.

In addition to these direct influences, our industrial system has been molded by passing fads and fancies, which have been varyingly worthwhile. A cover story appearing in *Business Week* described some of the "hot" management tools that have been presented to an ever-huntry executive group in the last few decades: the 1950s brought us Theory Y, Management by Objectives, and Diversification; the 1960s produced T-Groups, The Managerial Grid, and Matrix Management; in the 1970s we began to hear about Zero-Based Budgeting, Portfolio Management, and the Experience Curve; and now, in the 1980s, we're learning about Theory Z, Corporate Cultures, and One-Minute managing.[9]

The current industrial format is an altered classical system, a mechanistic model with some humanistic overtones and a partial scientific base. This evolved form is clearly evident at the operative or working levels of American corporations. The managerial and professional classes of these organizations, however, are less rigidly structured, although they are still constrained by the needs of the entity and the individual employees to survive and prosper. Such discrepancies within the same organization result in classic labor-management conflicts. Company loyalty decreases as one moves from the executive down to the operative level. With no guaranteed lifetime employment and job mobility the norm, job loyalty as found in a Japanese Nenko company is almost nonexistent in American companies, with the exception of a few firms, such as IBM, Hewlett-Packard, and Pitney Bowes, and among a new breed of relatively high-paid blue- and gray-collar workers.

Rogers claims that there is a continuing battle in the United States between labor and management over who should define work and how, resulting in strikes, slowdowns, and lockouts over hours, wages, and productivity. Overall, he feels the concept of hard, systematic work has won out, bringing with it job specialization, increasing discipline, intensified pace, and, most importantly, a clear-cut distinction between the individual's work and leisure times.[10]

It is ironic that the system that has evolved in the United States produced and still produces enormous quantities of goods and services at the cost of the social conditions under which the work ethic once flourished. The American dream of independence, individualism, and upward social mobility, earned through hard, productive work, has been diminished by the magnitude of the workplace itself. Labor is controlled by machine-paced work. company and union policies, rules, regulations, and standard operating procedures. Workers are motivated by the promise of rewards for their efforts and the fear of dismissal—a modified carrot-and-stick approach. This system serves the needs of business, since it can accommodate economic fluctuations brought on by changes in technology, world trade conditions, recessions, depressions, mergers and acquisitions, and divestments. Obviously, the hiring and firing of personnel based on downturns and upturns in the economy cannot breed employee loyalty, but it does result in a large, external pool of trained labor that can be tapped on relatively short demand. In addition to the flow of people between firms and industries prompted by business level fluctuations, the stream is augmented by individuals seeking increased rewards and opportunities and by the relative ease of movement between companies.

Recently the system has been changing, perhaps radically, because of an economy that is rapidly moving from a manufacturing to a service base. The workers in these new industries are generally higher paid and better educated than were their parents. Their loyalties to the unions their fathers helped create have begun to waiver and, in many cases, have disappeared altogether, transferred to the group they perceive they are dependent on—their company. As Brody insightfully states, these people are not anti-union, but rather indifferent to unions in general—a problem far more difficult for modern-day union leadership to overcome.[11] These new workers also appear to be willing to forgo job security, relocating if necessary, for opportunities to perform more interesting and challenging work, although they are willing to stay put and become loyal, dedicated employees if a company meets their needs. The basic American industrial model, however, largely remains a modified mechanistic dichotomy, although the previous sharp divisions between the classes have begun to blur.

NOTES

1. D. T. Rogers, "The American Work Ethic: Big Myth or Big Motivation?" in *The Straits Times* (Singapore), August 22, 1981.

2. Frederick W. Taylor, *The Principles of Scientific Management* (New York: W. W. Norton, 1911), 36–37.

3. Richard Edwards, *Contested Terrain: The Transformation of the Workplace in the Twentieth Century* (New York: Basic Books, 1979).

4. Tom Juravich, *Chaos on the Shop Floor: A Worker's View of Quality, Productivity, and Management* (Philadelphia: Temple University Press, 1985).

5. Robert K. Merton, "Bureaucratic Structure and Personality," *Social Forces* 18 (1940).

6. Victor A. Thompson, ed., *Modern Organization* (New York: A. A. Knopf, 1961).

7. Norma M. Williams, Gideon Sjoberg, and Andrée F. Sjoberg, "The Bureaucratic Personality: An Alternative View," *Journal of Applied Behavioral Science* 16, no. 3 (1980): 393.

8. Henri Fayol, *General and Industrial Management*, trans. C. Storrs (Sir Isaac Pitman and Sons, 1949).

9. John A. Byrne, "Business Fads: What's In and What's Out," *Business Week*, January 20, 1986.

10. Rogers, *The American Work Ethic.*

11. Michael Brody, "Meeting Today's Young American Workers," *Fortune*, November 11, 1985.

3 THE AMERICAN TRANSITIONAL MODEL

Factories are closing all over the United States, only to reopen in countries such as Japan, Korea, Singapore, Mexico, and Brazil. The result is much local and national unemployment, leading to emotional breakdowns, family deprivation and dislocation, trade imbalances, and political and economic problems at home and abroad. American industry is experiencing massive economic and industrial disruptions. These tremors are being brought about by increased competition due to: (1) greater foreign manufacturing capabilities in America; (2) improved manufacturing capabilities in Japan, Korea, Southeast Asia, and third-world nations located in South America and elsewhere; (3) new, sophisticated technologies that are radically changing how products are processed and manufactured; (4) changes in how manufacturing and service organizations are structured; and (5) the disintegration of traditional labor-management relationships.

An example of what is happening was spelled out in a front page *New York Times* article by Nicholas Kristof describing the inroads South Koreans have made in the comparatively few years they have been in the American marketplace.[1] The Hyundai Excel automobile, introduced in February 1986, exceeded Mazda in sales by the following July, becoming the fourth best-selling imported car in the United States. In addition to exporting cars, Hyundai is selling quality computers in the United States at a basic price of $699. Lucky Gold Star opened an assembly plant in Alabama in August 1986 and expects to

23

produce up to a million microwave ovens a year. Samsung, another South Korean company, and Lucky Gold Star are both manufacturing a million television sets a year in American factories. These and other achievements by our trading partners have caused our trading deficit to soar.

At the present time (the last quarter of 1986), wholly owned or partly owned Japanese manufacturing and/or parts-assembly companies located in the United States number approximately 500, up from 240 in 1982 and steadily increasing. They range from Toyota manufacturing cars in Fremont, California, in partnership with General Motors, to the ownership and active management of some of America's most distinguished lines of women's clothing—such as Anne Klein—along New York's Fashion (7th) Avenue.

These are only the beginnings of our problems. The Japanese, sensing a remarkable opportunity to pass the United States as the world's leading economic power, are positioning themselves for an all-out attack. Using Great Britain and the United States as historic examples, they are making their move in the world's capital markets. Furthermore, taking advantage of the tremendous surplus monies generated from the imbalance in trade originating from their outstanding manufacturing capabilities, they are actively buying American stocks, bonds, notes, and real estate in an attempt to become the world's major exporter of capital. Japanese investments throughout the world are expected to exceed $150 billion by 1990—a substantial increase over their $32 billion investments in 1980—with most of the monies invested in the United States. As of the end of 1984, Japan was the world's second-largest exporter of capital, Great Britain being number one, a position we held before our ever-increasing deficits turned us into a debtor nation. At the end of 1983, Japan's net foreign assets were $37.2 billion; within two years they had skyrocketed to $74.3 billion. As of 1986, Japan had become the world's leading creditor nation. Eight percent of the $2-trillion American banking industry is owned by Japanese banks, which also happen to control 25 percent of British banking. It is astounding to learn that one-third of our tremendous national debt is financed by Nomura, a single Japanese security firm.[2]

To remain a competitive industrial world force, the United States is being forced to undergo revolutionary changes in its manufacturing technologies, processes, and personnel relationships. But manufacturing and economic statistical data show that our responses to these challenges have been slow, uncertain, and inadequate. For the first time in our history—July of 1986, to be exact—we imported twice as many goods and services as we exported, increasing our trade deficit to $18 billion, $2 billion higher than the previous record set in January 1986. Between 1982 and 1984, our imports of technologically intensive capital goods rose from 26 percent to over 40 percent. In the high-density semiconductor market, where we were the world's uncontested leader, our market share dropped from 70 percent in 1979 to 30 percent in 1984. And, most importantly, our nondefense manufacturing output has barely increased by 1 percent annually since 1979. Throughout the period 1973 to 1979, our growth in nondefense output was a healthy 3.5 percent.

What are the reasons for this turn of events? Why haven't many American manufacturers been able to keep up with their Japanese counterparts by producing quality competitive goods? The answers are as varied as those rendering the opinions. However, there is a consensus among academics and practitioners that we have not kept up in areas such as applied research and development, manufacturing techniques and processes, quality control, capacity utilization, capital investment, and labor-management relationships and arrangements.

Can we reverse the cycle? The answer is a hesitant yes, but time is not on our side. We must accelerate the pace of our learning, adapting, and changing. For us to recapture our commanding position in the industrial world, Japan will either have to commit several major blunders, which is highly unlikely, or we will have to learn to play the game with a new set of rules. We must be willing to update and refine our own skills, as well as co-opting the best of those technologies, processes, and personnel programs, Japanese or otherwise, that are compatible with our industrial and social environments.

INFLUENCES ON THE NEW MODEL

What progress have we made toward the development and application of a transitional American model? A discussion relevant to this subject, entitled "Japan in America," was featured in the July 14, 1986, issue of *Business Week*. It broached the possibility of a "Japan, U.S.A."—a concept that we Americans are sooner or later going to have to accept as reality. The Japanese are pouring ever larger amounts of investment capital into the country. Its investment, although only about $19 billion at the end of 1985, had tripled since 1980. According to Japan's Ministry of International Trade and Industry (MITI), Japan expects its investment in United States manufacturing to increase by 14.2 percent annually until the year 2000. That magnitude of investment would result in a tenfold increase over the amount invested in the early 1980s. MITI predicts this will create 840,000 new American jobs.

This massive influx of capital is spawning new Japanese industrial centers, aptly termed "Auto Alley" in the mid-South and "Silicon Forest" in the Northwest. The invasion appears to be generally welcomed by Americans, despite negative reactions. It portends increased productivity, reduced unemployment, and financial stability for many localities throughout the United States. However, if we are not careful, it could also mean a marked decrease in our economic independence.

Business Week poses the question: Will the United States take advantage of this encroaching phenomenon to "build a hybrid form of manufacturing that blends Japanese methods and capital with American ingenuity and drive"? The hybrid would be an amalgam of Japanese and American techniques, methodologies, and styles that is suited to our environment, ethics, and culture. In their American enterprises, the Japanese have found that it is impossible for them to duplicate, totally or sometimes even partially, the homogeneous work conditions found in Japan. Thus, they have adopted their business practices and work mores to our industrial scene. The paradigm that is emerging, the American Transitional Model, should therefore work equally well for American companies and for Japanese companies located in the United States. The employment of this framework by American industry could to a large extent help prevent the loss of major sections of our economy to Japanese control, permitting us to live and compete with them on our own and other turfs. If we reach that point, what Yoshitaka Sajima, vice president of Mitsui & Company (U.S.A.), says may yet prove true: "The U.S. and Japan are not just trading with each other anymore—they've become part of each other."

The key to this new framework is quality. In a manual we received from Owens-Corning Fiberglas Corporation, we found the following persuasive passage:

Quality is the single most powerful tool any business can employ to guarantee its survival and success in today's ultra-competitive markets. . . . However, statistics alone do not demonstrate the clear-cut advantages of quality as graphically as does the success of the Japanese in world markets. In more than three decades since the end of World War II, the Japanese have developed a national concentration on product quality. . . . By the middle 1970s they achieved and surpassed the level of product quality of the West. At the same time they have improved their product quality, their penetration—and in some cases domination—of world markets has increased and accelerated at a proportional rate. The message for Western business is abundantly clear.[3]

American industry must learn how to manufacture products that are fundamentally and predictably sound. To achieve this, they can look to new techniques and methodologies, such as statistical process control, forms of in-depth quality assurance, and just-in-time manufacturing. But before all these systems must come a drastic modification of personnel practices. When management recognizes that most workers know their own jobs better than anyone else and, given the chance, will gladly accept the responsibility for managing their own work, the specific systems a manufacturer wishes to impose can be implemented with relative ease.

We have a ready-made model at our disposal—those Japanese companies that have opened plants in the United States. Certainly, we can learn from their methods, as well as from the techniques of Japanese companies in general. But are these systems really Japanese? According to most of the firms that replied to our letter of inquiry (see Appendix), the answer is an emphatic no. In fact, our use of the term "Japanese techniques" caused a small furor—many of our respondents devoted a great deal of space to driving home the point that these methodologies are not, in fact, Japanese in origin, but rather American techniques that the Japanese have adopted, adapted, and perhaps improved. This argument is supported by the few useful responses we received from Japanese companies operating in the United States. Kaneo Itoh, executive vice president of Mitsui & Co. (U.S.A.), reminded us in the first paragraph of his letter, "I am sure you are aware that Japan originally learned most of these techniques from the West."[4] Ken Esaki, vice president of Enplas (U.S.A.), prefaced his description of their management practices with the observation, "while we have many Japanese management techniques in the organization, many are not so different from those used by American companies."[5]

AT&T's Division Manager of Work Relationships and Corporate Culture firmly adheres to this point of view. He believes that his company's Quality of Work Life activities are not and should not be considered the implementation of Japanese management techniques, even though there are some conceptual similarities.[6] The General Counsel of Worthington Industries said his company has never studied Japanese methods, stating, rather, that many of the techniques and organizational ideas incorrectly labelled "Japanese" have been practiced by his company since it began in 1955.[7] The response from Hershey Foods Corporation similarly indicated that so-called Japanese business practices have been in use there since its founding in the early 1900s, long before the Japanese were singled out for the efficacy of their techniques.[8] While the Senior Vice President and General Counsel of GAF Corporation believes that most companies in the United States have not consciously implemented Japanese business techniques, he concedes that they have become part of the thought process of every American businessman due to the publicity they have received.[9]

Dennis W. Butt, director of manufacturing engineering at Outboard Marine Corporation, goes even further, writing that the current fascination with Japan "implies, at least, that we are inept or second-rate with respect to our counterparts in Japan, when the fact of the matter is that we are still, by far, the best manufacturing people in the world." At Outboard, he claims, the systems have been adopted "not because [they] have an oriental aura, but because to the U.S. manufacturing professional, they are fundamental to the effectiveness of our profession."[10]

SUMMARY

There is undoubtedly much truth in the premise that what many assume are Japanese innovations, ideas, and techniques are really translated American and Western European concepts. We believe, however, that at this stage of the game, when we are undergoing severe industrial problems that are taxing our economic viability, it is irrelevant who takes the credit. It is far more important that we start producing increased quantities of quality products at competitive prices throughout our entire manufacturing range, however the means, in order to maintain and augment our share of the domestic and foreign markets. It is to be hoped that we will then be able to reduce our huge negative trade balances and increase our nondefense manufactured output above the pitiful 1 percent it has risen annually since 1979.

Our research has indicated that our manufacturing and possibly our service sectors are already experiencing the beginnings of a new industrial model—one based on Western and/or American business concepts, techniques, processes, and methodologies that were exported by us to Japan, readily accepted and improved upon there, and then absorbed by the Japanese into their unique homogeneous society. After modifications, minor and major, they are now being re-exported to us as the Japanese manufacturing model, to be reabsorbed and redeveloped into a new and different format.

A starting point in the development of this model is the recognition that the United States and Japan are both economically sucessful democracies, with certain marked similarities, but many equally distinct differences.

Obviously, a direct transferal of the Japanese model to our industrial environment and culture is neither desirable nor possible. There is no reason, however, that we cannot assimilate key, workable components from their model (or any other usable model) into our own basic framework.

Based on our research, we have defined the model in terms of the following components:

1. It must satisfy and be compatible with our individual, group, cultural, and environmental needs.
2. It must be flexible enough to be based on our traditional manufacturing model, while being able to absorb the best and most useful elements of other industrial models, especially that of the Japanese.
3. It need not guarantee lifetime employment, but should make provisions for long-term employment, so that companies can justify heavy economical investment in the training of their employees.
4. It does not need to adopt a strict generalist approach, but rather should blend specialists with generalists.

5. It need not mandate the loss of individualism, but should provide corporate support for voluntary team formations.
6. It does not have to become the primary provider of recreational and cultural activities for its employees, but should encourage its people to engage voluntarily in joint outside activities.
7. It should adopt all programs that have proven efficient and effective for others, such as just-in-time manufacturing, flexible manufacturing systems, and state-of-the-art quality control processes.
8. It must provide our manufacturing sector with the means to produce high-quality, competitively priced products.

Parts II, III, and IV address in detail the specifics of the model, such as just-in-time manufacturing, quality control processes and forms of quality circles, and employee involvement and motivation, supported by case studies of some companies that have already begun to implement these concepts.

NOTES

1. Nicholas Kristof, "Low-Priced Cars and Electronics from South Korea Flooding U.S.," *New York Times*, 31 August 1986.
2. David Brunstein, "When the Yen Leaves the Sky It May Capture the Earth," *New York Times*, 3 September 1986.
3. M. G. Griffith, vice president of R&D, Owns-Corning Fiberglass Corporation, Technical Center, Granville, Ohio, letter and manual sent to authors, December 16, 1985.
4. Kaneo Itoh, executive vice president, Mitsui & Co. (U.S.A.), Inc., New York, N.Y., letter to authors, January 14, 1986.
5. Ken Esaki, vice president, Enplas (U.S.A.) Inc., Smyrna, Ga., letter to authors January 23, 1986.
6. Dr. Tapas K. Sen, AT&T, New York, New York, letter to authors, December 20, 1985.
7. Dale C. Brinkman, general counsel, Worthington Industries, Inc., letter to authors, January 2, 1986.
8. L. Philip Rothermel, director of productivity improvement, Hershey Foods Corporation, Hershey, Penn., letter to authors, December 16, 1985.
9. Edward E. Shea, senior vice president and general counsel, GAF Corporation, Wayne, N.J., letter to authors, July 21, 1986.
10. Dennis W. Butt, director of manufacturing engineering, Outboard Marine Corporation, Waukegan, Ill., letter to authors, February 18, 1986.

THE JUST-IN-TIME SYSTEM

4 THE JUST-IN-TIME SYSTEM OF PRODUCTION

When the oil crisis of the 1970s came along, Japan was particularly hard-pressed because of the scarcity of its natural resources. Reducing the labor force would have seemed to anyone else the obvious cost-saving measure, but not for the Japanese, with their long-established commitment to the lifetime employment system. Not surprisingly, a rapid decline in Japanese industrial productivity relative to the rest of the industrial world was the outcome.

It was during this period of economic turmoil that the just-in-time system of production management started to develop. While most Japanese companies were struggling to overcome losses resulting from the 1973 oil crisis, Toyota, to everyone's amazement, reaped an excessively large profit. Taiichi Ohno, former Vice President of the Toyota Motor Corporation and father of the just-in-time system, was, in large part, responsible for this growth. In search of survival (and, with luck, profits), many other Japanese companies looked to Toyota to discover what exactly it was that they were doing right. The revolutionary production management methods developed at Toyota eventually enabled Japanese industry to surmount the disastrous effects of the oil crisis and grow to become a model of efficiency for the rest of the industrialized world. The just-in-time system made its debut, eventually taking a leading role in many manufacturing environments located throughout the United States.

The Japanese had so few alternatives available to cut costs during the oil crisis years that inventory minimization seemed to be a logical approach. Americans, on the other hand, viewed inventory as an asset. During most of the 1970s, inflation soared above short-term interest rates, resulting in inexpensive carrying costs and the potential for greater future profits. Once interest rates started to rise and inflation started to fall, however, inventory became an expensive luxury that few could afford, and American industry recognized that the Japanese system of inventory management was well worth emulating.

THE JAPANESE SYSTEM OF PRODUCTION MANAGEMENT

The major principle behind the just-in-time system is the elimination of excess inventory by producing or procuring parts, subassemblies, and final products only when, and in the exact amounts, they are required. Unnecessary work-in-process and final inventories are decreased substantially. Typical Japanese plants operate on production schedules fixed weeks ahead of time, with little or no room to alter schedules and amass unwanted inventories.

One of the prerequisites of just-in-time manufacturing is a reduction in machine setup times. Traditionally, inventory build-up has been justified due to the time required to set up certain pieces of equipment for production runs (six hours to set up 800-ton presses was not unusual in the past). As long as American industry could profit from inventory, infrequent setups and long production runs were acceptable and unquestioned. But the Japanese never prized inventory the way Americans did; they thought it reasonable to produce items in small lots as needed if equipment setup times could be reduced. By 1970, after several years of engineering work, Toyota succeeded in decreasing to just three minutes the setup time of an 800-ton punch press used to form hoods and fenders. At present, Toyota workers can in many cases set up 800-ton presses in less than a minute.

One of the ways the Japanese reduced setup times was through the redesign of machinery and tooling. Dies are stored near the presses on roller conveyors, eliminating overhead cranes. Presses now have special guides that position the dies accurately before they are slid into place. At Toyota's hood-and-fender press operation, for example, dies quickly slide off the press and go into a waiting table as new dies are pushed into place from the other side.

Reducing the setup time of an 800-ton press to less than one minute is indeed a marvel of engineering. For the Japanese, however, such marvels are almost commonplace. While the American system has encouraged the training of lawyers, the Japanese believe that engineers are far more essential. They feel that lawyers merely fight over the division of the economic pie—engineers work to make it bigger. According to a report by the Office of Technology Assessment of the U.S. Congress, all high-school students are required to complete two years of mathematics and two years of science. Those who wish to attend college study mathematics each year, going beyond the level of trigonometry (most American high-school students stop at trigonometry, whether or not they plan to attend college). Since 1967, the number of engineers graduating from Japanese undergraduate programs has been rising. In 1981, for example, 75,000 engineers graduated from Japanese universities, while only 63,000 graduated in the U.S.—a remarkable differential, considering the Japanese population is only half that of the United States. Furthermore, many Japanese students who do not attend college go to technical, vocational, or semiprofessional schools that train them as support personnel for engineers and scientists in Japanese industry. It's no wonder that the Japanese have been able to develop their highly successful system of production management.

Japanese factories tend to focus on manufacturing a single product, part, or assembly, rather than attempting to produce all things for all people, as many American industrialists have often vainly hoped to do. In an article in the *Harvard Business Review*, professor Wickham Skinner described the conventional American factory as one that produces many products for numerous customers in a variety of markets, thereby demanding the performance of a multiplicity of manufacturing tasks all at once from one set of assets and people.[1] Not surprisingly, multiple goals, strategies, and policies channelled through a single manufacturing facility produce conflict, incoordination, and, ultimately, chaos. Japanese manufacturers have avoided this dilemma by maintaining simplicity through the focused factory.

The Japanese factory is generally operated by fewer than 750 employees. Many larger Japanese firms will break up a plant into these smaller manufacturing units. Small units foster greater communication between lower and upper management and are easier to manage. By concentrating on such units and specializing in a single part, product, or assembly, the Japanese master their trades, producing high-quality items at very low costs.

With this stress on specialization, the Japanese focused factory can utilize equipment geared to the production of particular items. Unlike many Western plants that use large multipurpose equipment, the typical Japanese plant will have several small, special-purpose machines developed by the company's own engineers and machinists. And, unlike their American counterparts, Japanese production workers are supported by extensive investments in equipment. Due to the Japanese practice of cross-training, Japanese workers can operate, for example, three machines rather than just one. Whereas in the traditional Western factory the worker must sit idly while his machine is operating, the Japanese worker can maintain and prepare for the next changeovers those of his machines not running while the others he handles are in operation. Yasuhiro Monden, a Japanese university Professor, has described this practice as a "multiprocess holding." In an *Industrial Engineering* article he describes how the design of multimachine processing has been beneficial for the Japanese:

1. The unnecessary inventory between each process can be eliminated.
2. The multi-process worker concept can decrease the number of workers needed, and thereby increase productivity.
3. As workers become multi-functional workers, they can participate in the total system of a factory and thereby feel better about their jobs.
4. By becoming a multi-functional worker, each worker can engage in teamwork, or workers can help each other.[2]

Monden authored *Toyota Production System: Practical Approach to Production Management*, which discusses in great detail how Toyota operates. In one section, he describes how each worker attends to the sixteen different machines in the gear-manufacturing process:

The laborer as a multi-function worker first picks up one unit of a gear brought from the preceding process and sets it on the first machine. At the same time, he detaches another gear already processed by this machine and puts it on a chute to roll in front of the next machine. Then, while he is walking to the second machine, he pushes a switch between the first and second machines to start the first machine. He performs a similar operation on the second machine, and then he moves to the third machine pushing a button again to start the second machine and so on, until he has worked on all 16 machines and finally returns to his initial process. This is done in exactly the cycle time necessary, perhaps, five minutes, so one unit of a finished gear will be completed in five minutes.[3]

By this method, only one stock item is produced as work-in-process by each machine, thus minimizing inventory and shortening production lead time. With a shorter production lead time, Toyota can quickly adapt to any changes in demand or customer orders.

The special-purpose machinery developed by company engineers and machinists is close to state of the art. The Japanese are reluctant to invest in equipment that has not been designed for their own individual use. According to one Japanese manager whose views were reported by Robert Hayes in a *Harvard Business Review* article: "Every machine represents a compromise among various users and, therefore, various uses. We prefer to design equipment that is directed toward our own needs. Not only do we get better equipment, but our costs are lower and our delivery times less."[4]

Self-made machines can reduce setup times to virtually nil. Because a machine has been designed with one particular job in mind, and all dies, fixtures, and so on have been built into the system, setups and changeovers simply require loading and unloading with no further adjustments. The use of small, special-purpose equipment has other advantages as well. Richard Schonberger, author of *Japanese Manufacturing Techniques* explains how it allows the Japanese more flexibility:

> If a need exists for making, say, 1000 parts per day, a Japanese company might have its toolmakers develop five small special-purpose machines, each with a capacity of around 200 parts per day; the Western company would probably buy one large high-priced multipurpose machine with a capacity in excess of 1000 parts per day. Smaller, self-made machines can run smaller lots of different parts, can be easily maintained one at a time, can be staffed variously, and can be added to (or dismantled or modified) one by one. By contrast, 'super-machines' tend to take on inordinate importance, so that whole lines, work schedules, and sales efforts are geared to their needs and limitations.[5]

Cross-training enables Japanese production workers to treat their machines with the respect due a fine watch. Every day they carefully check their machines to make sure they are in proper working order before starting operations. To the Japanese worker, who aims for the highest quality, daily machine maintenance is an automatic precaution to avoid the defects caused by faulty machines.

Many Japanese factories also use comprehensive equipment-monitoring and early-warning systems to check process flow, alert the operator when jams occur, measure dimensions and other characteristics of parts, and indicate when the tolerance limits of these characteristics are being approached. These systems also record the frequency with which tools and dies are used to make strokes, shots, or impressions and indicate when they should be adjusted or reground. With these monitoring systems, Japanese workers can easily supervise several machines at once.

Other equipment monitoring systems found in the Japanese factory further serve to increase productivity and control against defects. In Japan, these systems are known as *autonomation* and Yo-i-don.

The just-in-time system requires a smooth flow of parts in the production process, so delays must be avoided. Those delays caused by defects in the production process are minimized by the process of autonomation, which automatically or manually identifies defects throughout the assembly line.

In the automatic version of autonomation, devices embedded along the production line automatically identify defective items. Once a defect is sensed, a red light, called an *Andon*, flashes, alerting the work force to the source of the problem. While the light is flashing, the machining or assembly line stops and all employees within the vicinity of the problem are responsible for correcting the defect.

In the manual version of autonomation, employees inspect the work of those who precede them on the assembly line and turn on the Andon if they notice a defect. The machining or assembly line remains shut down until the defect is corrected by however many workers are needed to solve the problem.

Yo-i-don translates from Japanese as "ready, set, go" and is a process that coordinates the production of two or more parts required for assembly in succeeding production stages. The objective of Yo-i-don is to assure a timely completion of parts to minimize production delays.

To visualize Yo-i-don in action, suppose there are three operations, *A, B,* and *C,* which produce parts used in assembly by operation *D.* Operations *A, B,* and *C* have cycle times of ten, twelve, and fifteen minutes, respectively. Each worker engaged in each operation pushes a button upon completion of his job. If any of the three operations should take longer than fifteen minutes (the cycle time determined by the longest operation), then the Andon will flash at the work stations of those operations that have not yet been completed. Thus, everyone in the vicinity will be alerted that a worker or workers require assistance to avoid further delays in production.

Autonomation and Yo-i-don work well in the Japanese factory because of teamwork and job rotation. Each worker is familiar with many functions and machine operations and so can assist in times of trouble. The emphasis is on the achievement of the team, not the accomplishments of the individual. Consequently, the Japanese employee seeks to maximize the overall output of his group through his own individual efforts.

JUST-IN-TIME PURCHASING

The Japanese rely on small lot purchases to minimize inventory levels. Just-in-time in purchasing means frequent orders and frequent deliveries from the supplier, often several a day. Shipments consist of the exact quantities requested; large variances are not tolerated. Quite often, boxes or crates that accommodate a standard number of items are used as a control against under- or overshipments. An added benefit of just-in-time purchasing is the ease with which defects can be detected in the small shipments.

For any one particular part, Japanese companies prefer to purchase from a single source. Often the buying firm will purchase all of its vendors' output—a form of subcontracting. Japanese managers shun the practice of shopping around for better prices. In their view, the maintenance of steady, long-term relationships with their vendors is much more prudent. Such relationships foster loyalty among the suppliers; they become attuned to their buyers' needs for quality and reliable deliveries. The vendors also benefit in their turn from just-in-time inventory control since they themselves can produce in steady increments rather than in large batches.

Buyers and vendors in Japan enjoy a singular advantage: geographical proximity. Frequent, small shipments can be economically justified since the distances between buyers and suppliers are short. The buyer's engineers and quality-control experts can also visit the vendors frequently and work closely with them to resolve problems in the design or manufacturing stage. Should a vendor quote a price that's too high, the buyer can carefully review the specifications in person with the vendor to find out where the highest costs are and come up with ways to reduce them.

Japanese companies also work more closely with shipping handlers than their American counterparts. Just-in-time purchasing requires reliable deliveries—goods that arrive too early or too late can create havoc. Transportation systems generally concentrate instead on optimizing the use of drivers and storage spaces. Many Japanese traffic managers now schedule not only outbound freight (the sole function of most American traffic managers) but inbound freight as well. In this way, they can assure that incoming deliveries arrive on time.

PRODUCTION-LINE INVENTORY CONTROL AT TOYOTA

At the Toyota Motor Company, the just-in-time system of inventory control relies upon *Kanbans*, or cards, to communicate production requirements from the final point of assembly to the preceding operations that manufacture the assemblies, subassemblies, and parts that constitute the final product. Most Japanese plants operate the just-in-time system in a repetitive manufacturing environment.

Toyota uses two types of Kanbans in production planning: one for ordering production and the other for withdrawal. As an example of how they function, suppose that three products, X, Y, and Z, are being made on an assembly line. Parts x and y, required to produce these products, are stored behind the machining line where they are manufactured. Both of these parts are in boxes with attached production-ordering Kanbans. Each box contains a standard number of parts.

Part x is required for the assembly of product X. An operator from the assembly line that makes product X will go to the machining line, taking with him a number of withdrawal Kanbans equal to the number of boxes of part x he needs to make product X. When he picks up the number of boxes of part x required, he detaches their production-ordering Kanbans and returns to the assembly line with both the parts and the withdrawal Kanbans. He then detaches these withdrawal Kanbans and places them in the withdrawal Kanban file.

(Withdrawal Kanbans are also known as conveyance Kanbans because they are conveyed from the work station that uses the part to and from the work station that produces the part.)

The production-ordering Kanbans left behind at the machining line signal the operator there to replenish his supply of part x by as many boxes as there are Kanbans. These production-ordering Kanbans never leave the work station that produces the boxes of parts to which they're attached.

Toyota has developed a formula to determine the number of withdrawal and production-ordering Kanbans that should be in circulation for any particular part. The formula they developed is as follows:

$$ n = [D(T_p + T_w)a]/m , $$

where n is the number of production-ordering and withdrawal Kanbans in circulation,

D is the production requirements in units per shift,

T_p is the processing time for production requirement D, measured in terms of shifts,

T_w is the delay time for changeover setups and transportation, measured in terms of shifts,

a is a policy variable whose value is greater than zero (generally, a has a value of about 1), and

m is the number of units per container, usually less than 10 percent of D.

Using the above formula, the maximum inventory that is in circulation between two operations is determined by mn.

Obviously, by reducing the production lead time ($T_p + T_w$) or the policy variable a, the maximum inventory in circulation can be decreased. Because the Japanese are firmly committed to companywide quality control, the production processing time (T_p) is reduced as the proportion of quality goods produced increases. And, because the Japanese make continuing attempts to lower setup costs, the delay time (T_w) is reduced as well. Thus, Toyota has been able to lower the number of Kanbans in circulation as maximum inventory levels decrease.

Toyota's Kanban system eliminates the need to track the inventory position continuously. The initial inventory position at any one work station is equal to the number of containers at that station, all of which contain the same number of parts, times the number of parts within each container, with none on order. Every time a container is withdrawn from the work station, the detached production-ordering Kanban indicates the amount that is on order. The total of this amount on order plus the remaining parts in the unwithdrawn containers always equals the initial inventory position. As a result, the inventory position of any one part is always known.

CONCLUSION

Just-in-time production is not merely a system that reduces inventory. Japanese companies have realized several benefits from adopting the just-in-time system, among them, improved quality. With low levels of inventory on hand, finished products are much more visible, and defects are noticed more quickly and easily. As a result, quality problems can be attacked before they escalate to unmanageable proportions. Labor hours for rework are decreased, less material is wasted, and output rates are smoother. Low levels of inventory also shorten production lead times, which enables a firm to respond more readily to product and quantity changes, as well as forecast demand more accurately.

Japanese companies have not been the only ones to profit from successfully implementing the just-in-time system. Just-in-time production, as translated by our changing industrial manufacturing system, has already worked wonders in America for those organizations willing to commit the necessary resources to adapt the techniques to their systems.

NOTES

1. Wickham Skinner, "The Focused Factory," *Harvard Business Review* 52, no. 3 (May–June 1974): 113–21.
2. Yasuhiro Monden, "What Makes the Toyota Production System Really Tick," *Industrial Engineering* 13, no. 1 (January 1981): 39.
3. Yasuhiro Monden, *Toyota Production System: Practical Approach to Production Management* (Norcross, Ga.: Industrial Engineering and Management Press, 1983), 70.
4. Robert H. Hayes, "Why Japanese Factories Work," *Harvard Business Review* 59, no. 4 (July–August 1981): 64.
5. Richard J. Schonberger and James P. Gilbert, "Just-in-Time Purchasing: A Challenge for U.S. Industry," *California Management Review* 26, no. 1 (Fall 1983): 142–43.

5 CASES IN THE JUST-IN-TIME SYSTEM

OMARK INDUSTRIES

Omark Industries, a diversified manufacturer of equipment for harvesting timber and pulpwood, expendable products for gun sportsmen, and specialty fasteners, and a major supplier of cutting chain to the world's chain-saw producers, was one of the pioneers of just-in-time manufacturing in American industry. The company has twenty-one manufacturing plants, none unionized, located throughout four different countries. Even prior to developing its corporatewide program known as ZIPS (Zero Inventory Production System), Omark Industries had involved its employees in participative management to a considerable degree since its founding thirty-eight years ago. They have also steadily employed statistical quality-control procedures since 1959.

The origins of ZIPS can be traced to 1981, when Jack Warne, then executive vice president and now Omark's president, visited Japan. The following excerpts from a speech he made following his trip reveal his impressions of Japanese efficiency:

In October of 1981 I joined twelve other American executives on a trip to Japan. Our mission was to study the reasons for Japan's remarkable achievements. We visited twelve large Japanese manufacturing plants and spent a full day in each. We discussed management philosophy with the Japanese managers and toured the plants to see their methods in operation. As a result of what I saw on that trip, I very quickly lowered my assessment of our own company's performance in the area of human-resource management. I quite suddenly lost my complacency about our invincibility as a manufacturer. Quite frankly, I received a shock when I saw how advanced the Japanese were at managing their people and in their manufacturing methods.[1]

Warne does not credit the popular notion that the desire to work hard and succeed is a characteristic peculiar to the Japanese. As Warne sees it, "Japanese managers created a climate within their companies that satisfied the needs of their workers, that turned on the great power of cooperation and produced the unbeatable team spirit." He believes that anybody, anywhere, given the proper environment, will strive for the best, a conclusion supported by his discovery of team spirit not only at Toyota, Honda, and Fujitsu but also at Hewlett-Packard, IBM, and Delta Airlines. In his opinion, this spirit is the key to success, the essential force behind the more definable procedures that can improve productivity.

A new system such as ZIPS could not work without the commitment of all the workforce. To foster that commitment, Omark's management defined some indispensable guidelines:

- Treat people like intelligent human beings.
- Never place anyone in a position where their dignity is compromised.
- Treat everyone with respect.
- Allow employees to become involved in the pursuit of the company's goals.
- Train employees thoroughly for their jobs.
- Present employees with a clear and common goal.
- Make employees feel secure and confident in their jobs.
- Allow employees to make a significant contribution to the organization.
- Assure employees that they will share some of the gains of a successful enterprise.

These precepts have guided Omark Industries in the implementation of its zero inventory production system. In January 1982, Omark Industries formed a study team, chaired by Mike Rowney, director of research and development, and including representatives from manufacturing, industrial relations and communications, and finance, to study the applicability of Japanese production methods at Omark. The existing literature on the just-in-time system, consultations with knowledgeable people in the field, and visits to several progressive companies in both the United States and Japan led the study team to the following conclusions by April of 1982:

1. The key to Japanese manufacturing superiority is an integrated system involving unprecedented levels of employee education and involvement, ZIPS and commitment to perfect quality.
2. The system will work at Omark, but must be introduced as an integrated approach, not as piecemeal programs. Top management must be willing to make a total commitment.
3. People involvement and participative management is well understood and practiced by leading companies in this country. ZIPS is just beginning and must be learned from the Japanese. Company-wide Quality Control, or Total Quality Control, is just beginning in the U.S., but the concepts and practices are taught by such authorities as Deming and Juran.[2]

Directions in Total Quality Control

Deming and Juran have been trying to tell American industry for thirty years that quality improves productivity, but until now nobody has paid them any mind. The Japanese did, though, and now they have a lot to tell us.

In his keynote address to the Juran Institute's IMPRO 84 Conference, Warne described the Japanese approach to Total Quality. One of the theories the Japanese have proved is known as the 40/30/30 rule. According to this rule, about 40 percent of all quality problems causing customer dissatisfaction result from poor product design and engineering. Thirty percent result from errors during the manufacturing process. The remaining 30 percent are due to purchasing defective materials, components, and parts from suppliers. Those 40 percent of the problems caused by poor product design and engineering can result from:

- misunderstanding the customer's needs,
- misunderstanding the end use of the product,
- errors in engineering,
- incorrect specifications,
- a design that is too difficult to manufacture, and
- use of inappropriate materials.

Problems in design and engineering can only be solved after obtaining feedback from the customer. One of the criteria used to determine the recipient of the Deming prize in Japan is the efficiency of a company's feedback system. Learning what the customers think of a product (how they use it, what they had expected from it, etc.) and responding quickly to this information helps guard against quality problems in design and engineering.

Quality problems due to errors in the manufacturing process can arise from any of the following:

- inadequate tooling,
- poorly maintained machines and tooling,
- inadequate machines,
- faulty measuring tools,
- inadequate instructions,
- sloppy work,
- inattention to detail, and
- lack of operator training.

Inspection will not solve problems resulting from errors in the manufacturing process. Only continual monitoring through statistical process control will identify the causes of defects.

Close relationships with fewer suppliers will reduce the likelihood of defective purchases. The 30 percent of quality problems that result from faulty supplies will diminish as the adversarial supplier/buyer relationships of the past cease.

Omark Industries' Three-Circle Approach

Based on what they learned from the Japanese, Omark developed their new three-circle approach to manufacturing, illustrated in Figure 5–1. Each of the three circles represents a major aspect of Omark's productivity program; together they symbolize Omark's new integrated model of operating efficiency. The top circle demonstrates Omark's firm conviction that the employee's involvement as partner in the enterprise is essential for success. Employee education plays a major role here, not to be underestimated. Omark committed $300,000 for educational purposes during the initial period of its new program's development, a large amount in the recessionary days of 1982, which could not have been more wisely spent.

While programs for training quality-circle members, leaders, and facilitators were being developed, the company sent reports of Jack

Figure 5-1. Omark Industries' Three-Circle Approach.

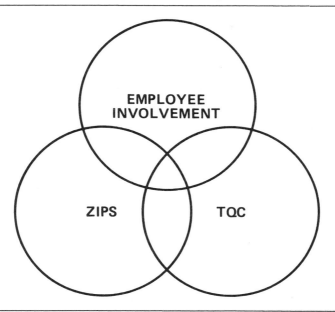

Source: Dave Pinch, "Corporate-Wide Implementation of ZIPS at Omark Industries (Zero Inventory Production System)" (Address given in Portland, Oregon, n.d.).

Warne's trip to Japan to all personnel through the corporate magazine. Omark's new Statement of Philosophy, stressing its strong commitment to employee involvement, quality, and ZIPS, was widely publicized throughout the organization. Once the news was spread, action was taken with full support from top management. What was known as the "Road Show" became the medium of communication for Omark's educational campaign. A corporate team led by Jack Warne travelled to each of Omark's plants to present two-day seminars on participative management, quality circles, and ZIPS. Lectures were followed by small group discussions on the advantages and problems that each plant might experience during the implementation phases of the program. Everyone participated—first-line supervisors, staff, clerical personnel, and hourly personnel all had their chance to learn about the new three-circle approach. The ground was laid for total quality control and ZIPS at Omark Industries.

Shortly afterward, groups, representing several functional areas, were formed at each plant to study ZIPS in detail. The only book then available, Shigeo Shingo's *Study of Toyota Production System from Industrial Engineering Viewpoint,*[3] was analyzed chapter by chapter and regularly discussed. Each team member led the discussion of one chapter, presenting its contents to the entire team. As a learning tool, this approach couldn't have been more effective. Not only was the Toyota production system learned in great depth, but several team members were able to offer innovative suggestions on how ZIPS could work within their plants. Some even took the initiative to improve setup times.

By January 1983, Omark was ready to implement ZIPS. ZIPS teams were appointed (with a leader or coordinator in most locations) to work on reducing inventory of a single product or product line. Efforts were made to decrease lot sizes, cut work-in-process inventory, and reduce lead time. To accomplish this, tooling changes had to be speeded up and machinery needed to be changed from a process-oriented to a product-oriented layout. At Omark, as in many Western plants, like machines were traditionally grouped together, with a product's travelling time from one department to another frequently taking anywhere from six to twelve weeks. ZIPS teams started to dismantle these groupings, placing different machines alongside one another, with little or no space for work-in-process inventory to build up. Operators found themselves next to the people who performed the other operations, instead of out of sight. Sequential operations could take place within minutes or seconds of each other instead of being separated by days.

Early results have been outstanding. A few weeks after the pilot projects began, productivity improvements were found to be as high as 30 percent in some areas, lot sizes had been reduced by 50 to 90 percent, lead times were shortened, and problems with quality were being detected much sooner. Because employees were being cross-trained to move from job to job, morale was up and enthusiastic ideas were pouring from the shop floor. Lot-size reductions revealed problems once buried in excess inventory that were being approached with newfound excitement.

Omark Industries knows that its ZIPS program is an ongoing process, requiring commitment to teaching personnel the basics of quality-circle problem-solving techniques, team building, value analysis, and managerial and supervisory training. In addition, reporting accomplishments and experiences with ZIPS, quality control, and employee involvement in the company's weekly newsletter keeps communication flowing throughout the organization. Omark also sponsors annual ZIPS conferences to encourage further employees' efforts. At these conferences, corporate, division, and plant management share information on ZIPS' progress. Each plant is given the opportunity to present its approach to implementing ZIPS and to describe its achievements. In addition, awards are given for success in the following categories: quality, small-lot manufacturing, shop-floor involvement, productivity, product-oriented plant layout, inventory reduction, customer service, fast tooling change, purchasing, and value analysis. Speeches by top management recognizing each plant's efforts further support the ZIPS program. According to Omark Industries, the annual conferences generate a fantastic cross-fertilization of ideas from plant to plant throughout the entire company.

To date, Omark's achievements with ZIPS prove that just-in-time manufacturing is alive and functioning well. As little as eighteen months after first learning about ZIPS, results at Omark's plants have been impressive. While companywide inventories were reduced by 34 percent and customer service improved throughout the entire organization—remarkable achievements in themselves—several plants made strides bordering on the extraordinary.

At their Onalaska plant in Wisconsin, which makes accessories for gun sportsmen, inventory of gun-cleaning rods was reduced by 94 percent, productivity was increased by 20 to 30 percent, and lead time was reduced from two weeks to one day. Operators, who now perform their own setups, instead of having them done by electrical or maintenance personnel, have succeeded in reducing setup time from forty-five minutes to six.

Employees at the Prentice, Wisconsin, plant, which makes log loaders for the timber industry, developed a product-oriented layout to make hydraulic valve-control handles. Using value analysis, they reduced the number of product configurations and eliminated some purchased parts. Single-piece production in the new layout reduced part-travel distance from 2000 feet to 18 inches, setup delays were eliminated, work-in-process inventory was reduced from sixty pieces to one piece, and lead times were shortened from thirty days to just a few minutes. The cost of $1,500 seemed well worth the projected annual savings of more than $8,000.

Omark's Mesabi, Minnesota, plant, which makes twist drills, was able to reduce inventory by 92 percent and cut scrap and rework by 20 percent. Lead times for manufacturing gun-cleaning kits were shortened from two weeks to one day. And changeover time for the presses that manufacture saw bars was reduced from about two-and-a-half hours to just two-and-a-half minutes. Lot sizes of reloading products were generally cut from 500 to 30, inventory was reduced by 50 percent, and lead times were shortened from six weeks to two days, resulting in a make-to-order business.

Despite these and other accomplishments throughout the organization, Omark Industries believes that the most impressive result of all has been the outstanding response of its employees at all levels to ZIPS. Omark has found that their openness to new concepts, willingness to tackle new jobs, insight, creativity, and enthusiasm have been the key to the company's success with ZIPS. Although the program is relatively new, Omark is convinced of its potential and is committed to its future. For Omark, ZIPS signifies improved customer service, lower costs, higher quality, and, most importantly, a motivated work force that doesn't cease to strive for constant improvement.

GENERAL ELECTRIC COMPANY

Just-in-time manufacturing is becoming a way of life at General Electric. About ninety-four GE locations have already initiated JIT methods, several of them confirming the tremendous benefits of just-in-time in customer service, quality, and productivity.

Many GE plants have been able to reduce total inventory by 40 percent in less than a year's time by shifting production from lot sizes of one week's worth to one day's worth. Even without considering a reduction in waiting time between operations, this can be easily achieved.

To illustrate this point, consider the following hypothetical situation: the weekly demand for a product is ten units, each requiring twelve two-hour operations. Slack time between operations is twenty hours. Assuming a one-shift operation, the advantages of producing daily rather than weekly lot sizes may be seen below: [4]

Weekly Lot Size (10 units)

Operation time: 12 opns. × 10 units × 2 hrs.	= 240 hrs.
Waiting time: 12 opns. × 20 hrs.	= 240 hrs.
Total time in hours	= 480 hrs.
Total time in weeks (480 hrs./40 hrs. per wk.)	= 12 wks.
Total inventory in process: 12 × 10	= 120 units

Daily Lot Size (2 units)

Operation time: 12 opns. × 2 units × 2 hrs.	= 48 hrs.
Waiting time: 12 opns. × 20 hrs.	= 240 hrs.
Total time in hours	= 288 hrs.
Total time in weeks (288 hrs./40 hrs. per wk.)	= 7.2 wks.
Total inventory in process: 7.2 × 10	= 72 units

Thus, by changing from weekly lot sizes to daily lot sizes, work-in-process inventory can be decreased from 120 to 72 units—a 40 percent reduction.

Actual results are even more impressive. At GE's Medical Systems Group in Milwaukee, over 1250 people have been trained in JIT concepts, and over 45 teams work together to solve the problems that are exposed as inventory levels are lowered. Kanbans are used to control the flow of materials between operations. Storage space that was as large as two tennis courts has been eliminated, lead times have been cut in half, and work-in-process inventory has been reduced by 50 percent.

Losses from quality problems and long lead times were common in the manufacture of water-cooled induction heating capacitators at GE's Capacitator Products Plant in Hudson Falls, N.Y. Just-in-time manufacturing has changed all that. The production area has been entirely redesigned so that all units now move smoothly from operation to operation rather than being produced in large batches at each work station. Production operators who were once specialized have been trained to handle a wide variety of tasks. One operator, for example, now performs winding, pressing, scrub soldering, assembling, welding, and testing for leaks. Plant managers have noticed the enthusiasm with which these employees have adopted their new duties. Just-in-time manufacturing at the Hudson Falls plant has brought about other significant improvements: [5]

- The distance travelled between operations has been reduced from 600 to 20 feet.

- The manufacturing cycle time has been reduced from three days to one hour.

- Work-in-process inventory has been reduced from 120 units to 10 units.

- Manufacturing losses due to quality problems have been reduced by 50 percent—the short cycle from assembly to testing permits much faster identification of quality problems, and the need to make extra coils as a buffer against possible failures has been eliminated.

- Customer delivery cycles have been cut by two weeks.

- Costs of supervision, material handling, and expediting have been reduced.

At GE's dishwasher manufacturing facilities in Louisville, Kentucky, a redesign of the work flow within the plant has eliminated about 50 percent of the conveyors required for handling materials. Point-of-use manufacturing is now in operation whereby parts are fabricated by automated presses right at the assembly line where they are used.

Throughout the assembly line, work stops in front of each operator and is released only when it is correctly completed. Every operator checks for quality, so defects are not allowed to proceed down the line.

Vendor certification programs have done away with the time-consuming incoming inspection process. Many purchased parts are now provided by vendors who have demonstrated their competence in producing quality parts. Bypassing inspection, these parts are delivered directly to the point where they will be used.

Thanks to just-in-time efforts at GE's dishwasher plant, market share has increased, service calls have been reduced by 60 percent and inventory turnover has increased by 200 percent.

General Electric believes that significant employee involvement and product quality are necessary prerequisites for successful implementation of a JIT system. A quick flow of materials from one operation to the next requires the highest levels of quality. All employees, not only managers and engineers, need to become more involved in manufacturing to help resolve the many problems that are exposed when cycle times are reduced for the first time, and must continue to monitor and improve quality after the system is in place.

Several GE managers who have been successful in implementing just-in-time programs have made the following recommendations:[6]

- Consider JIT as a concept, not a project to be scheduled and completed. Therefore, don't plan it to death. Start small and build on your successes.

- Make sure that the program focuses on a priority need of the business, otherwise JIT will soon fade from view.

- Early in the program, educate the hourly workforce in JIT. Develop their understanding of JIT, and get their involvement in solving the problems that are exposed. Be ready to accept some mistakes.

- Assure the understanding and commitment of the top manager on site before attempting a program like JIT that involves major changes from prior practices.

- Remember that JIT isn't a manufacturing program. It is the operating philosophy of the business. It challenges the total organization. Marketing and Engineering play vital roles in the scheduling and design decisions that impact on the ability to operate Just-in-Time.

THE XEROX CORPORATION

Managers at the Rank Xerox plant in Venray, the Netherlands, can easily extoll the merits of just-in-time manufacturing. Before the implementation of just-in-time concepts at the plant, Xerox's copier-manufacturing costs were 30 to 40 percent higher than those of its Japanese competitors. Today, the plant can produce copiers that remain cost competitive with the Japanese simply because inventories have been drastically reduced. The three-month supply of raw-material inventory worth $130 to $140 million carried in 1981 has been cut to a mere 0.8 month's supply, roughly valued at $33 million—a decrease of at least 75 percent. Xerox estimates that they save $20 million a year on inventory holding costs alone. Their materials-transport bill has decreased by 20 percent, and 30 percent less space is needed for warehousing because of the lowered inventories.

Xerox believes that just-in-time is an ongoing process of incremental improvement that must be supported by everyone from top management to the workers on the shop floor to achieve maximum effectiveness. Five major themes and a set of basics for achieving dramatic improvements, developed by consultant William Wheeler of Coopers & Lybrand, form the foundation of the company's just-in-time program and are described in its "Just-in-Time Manufacturing Survival Kit."[7]

Figure 5-2.   Steps for Achieving Dramatic Improvements: 5 Major JIT Themes.

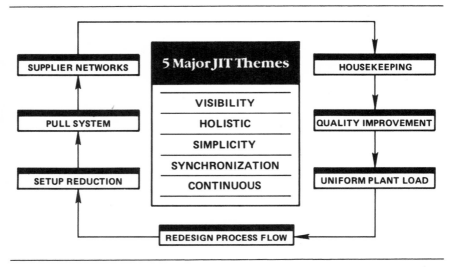

Source: Xerox Computer Services "Just-in-Time Manufacturing Survival Kit" (Los Angeles: Xerox Corporation, 1986).

The Five Major Underlying Themes

1. *Visibility*—Don't hide mistakes.

    According to Wheeler, the master schedule, production goals, and quality charts should be put out where everyone can see them. This way, the entire factory can keep track of any production that may be off schedule, as well as scrap rates that are too high, with the added plus that all lines of communication between workers and management are wide open. Problems in manufacturing are no longer hidden in excess inventory, resulting in unmanageable crises later on. Employees on the shop floor can productively engage in problem-solving activities, rather than attempting to pass the buck when it's too late.

2. *Holistic*—Let the workers solve problems.

    Wheeler describes holistic organizations as ones that "lasso these previously untapped resources [workers at the low level of the

organizational hierarchy] and attempts to solve as many problems at as low levels as possible, saving only the really tough ones
for their highly paid management heavyweights."[8] When the
workers at the bottom start to participate in brainstorming sessions, the organization's ability to produce timely solutions significantly increases.

3. *Simplicity*—Is there an easier way?
Methods of operation at each step of the manufacturing process
should be challenged to make sure that things are done right the
first time and that any one task does not merely correct the mistakes of a previous operation. Since people on the shop floor
know their jobs better than anyone else, they are the ones to
consult for ways to eliminate waste. Engineers should be called
in only as technical backup, not as problem solvers.

4. *Synchronization*—Make only what's needed now.
Finished goods should be produced in the amounts that satisfy
customer demand. Excessive production just to make full use of
machine capacity only leads to waste. Wheeler's advice:

> It's okay to operate at speeds lower than threshold, especially if some ma-
> chines are able to make parts much faster than they can be consumed. In
> fact, overall manufacturing flow is often slowed down to achieve full
> synchronization to both internal and external demand. A constant speed
> is established whereby different parts are churned out in a time-phased
> repetitive sequence and the sum total on completion of a run equals
> exactly the desired number of end items. There's no leftover or spares.[9]

5. *Continuous improvement*—Catch the overachievers syndrome.
Just-in-time inventory management means never being able to
say your goals have been met. Better and better results should
always be sought. Wheeler cites a classic example: reduce setup
time from two hours to four minutes, and then try to reduce it
to forty seconds. The challenges are always waiting to be met.

Basics For Achieving Dramatic Improvements

Surrounding the five major JIT themes in Figure 5–2 are the basic
steps Wheeler prescribes and Xerox follows to facilitate the just-in-

time process. On top of the list is housekeeping—putting one's own house in order is the first essential according to Xerox. Here's what Wheeler says:

> Stress that it's each individual's responsibility to put their setup tools away in the same location and order as before when they're done using them. Productivity increases when people no longer waste time scrambling around searching for the right tool. Clean broom award-winners aren't necessary. But reasonably good housekeeping habits throughout the factory instill a sense of pride. A clean factory floor void of litter, junk, and inventory serves as a constant reminder that the company's serious about being successful in its business. Operators must also feel personally responsible for maintaining their equipment in good condition, almost as if it's a second car. So they automatically wipe their machines down at the end of a shift and carefully check them over to see if any preventative maintenance needs to be performed. As a result, there's a lot less down time due to machine failures.[10]

The second basic step, quality improvement, cannot be emphasized enough—just-in-time manufacturing just won't survive without quality. Roughly 85 to 90 percent of all quality problems can be solved by the people on the shop floor; the rest need to be handled by quality-assurance experts. Xerox believes that, with the necessary tools and resources, the operators can keep the manufacturing process under control and perform their tasks correctly the first time around.

Wheeler states, "The idea is to move from process control to precontrol aimed at reducing variances in part numbers, setups, cycle times, quality, and so forth. Variation research techniques have proven extremely effective in pinpointing the root cause of problems. The ultimate objective, of course, is zero defects."[11] He goes on to say that fail-safing through automation is becoming an increasingly popular way to aim for zero defects. Mechanical functions are monitored through a series of checks and balances built into the system. Sensors can be installed that sound whenever the equipment malfunctions, reducing the possibility of producing a bad part. The condition can then be corrected and quality maintained.

Uniform plant load, effected by producing every single piece according to demand, is the third essential of just-in-time manufacturing. A cycle time for making each component should be established so that the flow of materials through production is synchronized with the sales rate. The flexibility to produce according to varying customer preferences on a daily basis can be easily attained by generating a little of everything every day. This way, any inaccuracies in forecasting can be compensated for by always having a variety of small lot sizes moving along the production line toward final assembly. Should a machine produce more pieces than needed, it should, of course, be run at a slower speed to avoid the accumulation of excess inventory.

Next on the agenda is a redesign of the process flow. The value of every step in the manufacturing process should be seriously questioned. As many operations as possible should be overlapped, and functional departments should be grouped using cellular manufacturing technology. Batch-processing wastes time and effort in moving, storing, tracking, and retrieving parts as needed. All this is avoided by producing one piece at a time, which also allows the people at each succeeding operation to better control for defects, incurring less waste as only one single piece is rejected.

In a cellular manufacturing environment, workers are positioned in the center of each cell. This way, they can move around the cell and manage several machines, using their spare time to prepare for the next machine changeover. Wheeler suggests that workers should identify and solve obstacles to setup reduction such as poorly designed tools and equipment. He also recommends that each setup be videotaped, clocked, and then analyzed to pinpoint areas for improvement. Continuous incremental improvements can reduce setup times by at least 75 percent, he claims.

In just-in-time manufacturing, parts are pulled through the system rather than pushed through. A fixed upper limit is predetermined, and a signal is developed to alert workers when items must be obtained from suppliers or preceding operations. The signal authorizes lower-level operations to make either one more piece or container's worth. Production stops whenever the replenishment signals cease.

Xerox consultants recommend the following to obtain vendor commitment to just-in-time goals: [12]

1. *Stress Quality*
   Ask vendors to send statistical quality-control charts with each shipment to confirm that the quality of parts delivered meets customer-imposed standards. When such statistical evidence is available, the company's receiving inspection department may be abolished, and incoming parts can go straight to the assembly line.

2. *Prevent Damage Enroute*

Conduct surveys to determine how goods are damaged during loading, unloading, and in transit. Hold damage-prevention sessions with external material handlers and transport-company personnel responsible for deliveries to the factory and finished products to the customer and ask them how to avoid future casualties. Combine their suggestions with the results of research on packing and handling techniques to devise better procedures. Develop training films and programs that motivate and teach external material handlers and transport-company employees to use these new methods. Monitor their performance and convince their management to assign only the most conscientious crews, who will take special pride in their work because they've been singled out as the best.

As a persuasive side effect, the shipping firms' insurance premiums may be lower, and their customers most certainly will be pleased that nothing's broken or marred when their shipments arrive.

3. *Negotiate Long-Term Contracts*

Agree to give the supplier a certain annual percentage of the company's business in return for guaranteed prices. After the price issue is settled, establish requirements for vendor performance, such as shorter lead times, more frequent and reliable deliveries, and smaller lot sizes.

In everyday practice, buy a fixed percentage of the supplier's capacity at the commodity level and firm up the specific part numbers at the last minute. If one supplier doesn't have enough capacity, split the difference proportionally with another vendor.

4. *Address the Lead Time Issue*

Bypass purchasing, receiving, and accounts payable and have the company's manufacturing operation deal directly with the vendor when more parts are needed. There's no need to provide a horizon beyond the supplier's manufacturing lead time, which may be only the twenty minutes it takes to build a part. Otherwise, too many shifts in forecast and demand transpire between the time the purchase order is issued and when the parts are actually received.

Figure 5-3. Significant Achievements Through JIT and Automation.

IN THE APPLIANCE AND TRANSPORTATION EQUIPMENT BUSINESS

Benefits	Gen'l Electric Appliances Louisville, KY Dishwashers	Gen'l Electric Erie, PA Locomotives	Gen'l Electric Evandale, OH Aircraft Parts	Westinghouse Bloomington, IN	Sanyo Japan Refrigerators
Inventory Raw Materials Slashed	60%	$900,000*	45%		
Labor Cut Direct Other	25%	$20,000*	15%		85%
Mfg. Lead Time Shortened	81%	94%**			
Capacity Expanded	20%				200%
Materials Stockouts Reduced				95%	
Profits Increased					729%
Quality Improved	53%				

*One Commodity Only   **Major Component

IN THE HIGH TECH INDUSTRY

Benefits	Hewlett-Packard Disc Memory Boise, ID	Datapoint Computers	Sykes Datatronics Terminals	Motorola
Inventory Slashed	50%	$19,200,000		$210,000,000
Labor Cut			20%	
Capacity Expanded			400%	
Materials Scrap Reduced	33%			
Profits Increased		100%*		

*Purchased Parts
Note: All figures shown here are based on published results from a collection of media sources.   (Figure 5-3. continued overleaf)

Figure 5-3. continued

IN THE AUTOMOTIVE INDUSTRY

Benefits	Gen'l Motors Corp-Wide	Gen'l Motors Cadillac Livonia, MI Engines	Gen'l Motors GMAD Hamtramck Car Assembly	Gen'l Motors Buick Flint, MI Car Assembly	Ford Engine Cleveland, OH Engines	Ford Corp-Wide	Chrysler Windsor Van Assembly	Japan Auto Ind.
Inventory Cut								
WIP	22%	29%			70%	27%		
Finished Goods		50%			42%			
Labor Slashed								
Direct				34%				60%
Indirect				34%				67%
Other				57%				
Setups Shortened								85%
Space Freed Up			32%	55%				50%
Capacity Expanded							54%	
Materials								
Freight Reduced				$48/Car				
Total Costs Saved				$484/Car				
Quality Improved				$50/Car				

IN MISCELLANEOUS MANUFACTURING PLANTS

Benefits	Int'l Harvester Springfield, OH Heavy Trucks	Harley-Davidson Motorcycles	AP Auto Parts Toledo, OH	Stanodyne Engine Comp.	Harris Corp. Ft. Worth, TX Printing Equip.	LTV Vought B-1 Parts
Inventory Decreased	83%*	75%				
Direct Labor						
Cut				20-50%	67%	65%
Mfg. Lead Time						
Diminished					88%	
Setups Shortened		75%				
Capacity Expanded			67%			
Materials						
Freight Reduced	$137,000*					
Total Cost Saved		$700–1000/unit				
Quality Improved		24%			94%	

*Engines Only   Note: All figures shown here are based on published results from a collection of media sources.

Source: Xerox Computer Services, "Just-in-Time Manufacturing Survival Kit" (Los Angeles: Xerox Corporation, 1986).

Figure 5-4. Your Potential Just-in-Time Paybacks.

	Automotive Components	Flexible Packaging	Electrical Cons. Goods	Mechanical Equipment	Fashion Goods
	Repetitive	Process	Repetitive	Job Shop	Repetitive
Manufacturing Lead Time Reduction	89%	86%	85%	83%	92%
Productivity Increase					
Direct	19%	50%	n/a	5%	29%
Indirect/Salary	60%	50%	38%	21%	
Scrap/Rework Reduction	50%	63%	26%	33%	61%
Purchased Material Price Reduction	n/a	7%	n/a	6%	11%
Inventory Reduction					
Raw Material	35%	70%	50%	73%	70%
Work-in-Process	89%	82%	85%	70%	85%
Finished Goods	61%	71%	90%	0	70%
Setup Reduction	75%	75%	94%	75%	91%
Space Reduction	53%	n/a	80%	n/a	39%
Capacity Increase	n/a	36%	n/a	n/a	42%

Source: Xerox Computer Services, "Just-in-Time Manufacturing Survival Kit" (Los Angeles: Xerox Corporation, 1986).

Reduced lead time and lower costs are directly related, so there's plenty of incentive to get the vendors operating in a JIT environment with a supportive MRP II (materials requirements planning) system. MRP II, computerized and based on forecasts, lists parts required for assembly and when they should be available for assembly.

5. *Build a Solid Relationship of Trust*
   Create a situation where the company can always depend on the vendor and vice versa. A larger share of the firm's business means greater profits for the vendor and lower prices for the customer. Encourage the vendor to reinvest those profits in further improvements.

William Wheeler believes that job shops, repetitive manufacturers, and process environments alike have a great deal to gain from just-in-time manufacturing; even diverse nonmanufacturing operations like banks and hospitals have derived significant benefits. Wheeler argues that any company that considers itself unique will eventually find itself uniquely out of business.

Figures 5–3 and 5–4 certainly appear to corroborate his faith in the just-in-time system.

WHIRLPOOL CORPORATION

In early 1982, the Whirlpool Corporation decided to convert their Kitchen Products Division plant in Findlay, Ohio, to just-in-time manufacturing. A J-I-T Task Force was formed of representatives from materials, procurement, quality control, and manufacturing from four different plants. Several programs were designed to educate everyone involved in the new undertaking. Within just a few months, just-in-time delivery and production techniques were in operation.

Whirlpool's Findlay plant manufactures 5,500 dryers, dishwashers, and ranges per day on three production lines. Approximately 380 suppliers deliver to the plant. With just-in-time, Whirlpool maintains an average of a three-and-a-half day supply of parts and materials from each of these suppliers.

At Whirlpool, the just-in-time system primarily depends upon inbound transportation, communications, and quality control. Since 99 percent of the Findlay plant's inbound shipments are sent by truck, all trucking arrangements needed to be modified. The company's traffic supervisor, Bill Ryder, worked out a new arrangement with its contract carrier, Signal Delivery, establishing "bid runs," whereby the carrier's drivers would, in effect, be on lease to the Findlay plant. Under this arrangement, parts supplied from vendors as far away as Knoxville and Nashville, Tennessee, are delivered by individual "bid drivers." These bid drivers pick up shipments from vendors in their assigned specific geographic areas and deliver them to Whirlpool. Shipments from vendors farther away from the Findlay plant, however, such as those in New York City or Boston, are transported to the plant by common carriers. Out of the sixty trucks that arrive daily at the plant, approximately half are driven by Signal's bid drivers.

Good communication with the carriers is an important prerequisite to maintaining the just-in-time system. In early 1984, Bill Ryder presented an educational program entitled "Meeting the J-I-T Challenge" to sixty-five trucking officials from twenty-two companies, during which he explained the just-in-time system and how it lowers inventory costs, improves product quality, and eliminates waste in production. Ryder further stressed that product quality is a major factor in the J-I-T program, noting how transportation plays a vital role by adhering to delivery deadlines, correct freight handling techniques, and consistency in transit times. Soon after Ryder's presentation, several letters followed from carriers expressing their appreciation in being able to participate in the program.

The second essential ingredient of Whirlpool's J-I-T system, good internal communications, is being fostered by the Total Communications Program and a divisionwide Work-In-Process Task Force. The Total Communications Program provides the means to exchange knowledge, experiences, and ideas on J-I-T at Whirlpool. Information is disseminated by way of a daily plant newspaper, a quarterly publication, regular department supervisor meetings, supervisor round tables, and regularly scheduled meetings between the divisional vice president, his staff, and the plant's employees.

Whirlpool's divisionwide Work-In-Process Task Force is comprised of representatives from all manufacturing functions, who meet monthly to discuss procedures in operation at the plant. Typical topics include ways to reduce inventories further, make quicker plastic mold and die changes, improve preventive maintenance on production equipment, and respond more rapidly to machine breakdowns.

Quality control is the third ingredient in J-I-T's success. Whirlpool instituted a Total Quality Assurance program with its suppliers in order to increase the likelihood of receiving parts that conform to acceptable quality standards, thus shortening inspection time. Where inspection was once the order of the day, prevention is now the rule. Roughly 80 percent of Whirlpool's parts are supplied by vendors on Whirlpool's Source Assurance Program, who have proven records of shipping high quality products. Those parts supplied from uncertified vendors are inspected through functional tests, visual tests for color and other aesthetic values, and hardness readings for paints.

Whirlpool's Source Assurance Program seeks to identify problems suppliers may have in satisfying Whirlpool's quality standards. Should a supplier's parts be substandard, he or she is required to submit a plan of action detailing how and when the problem will be corrected. If corrective action is taken, such suppliers may be accepted into the program.

Whirlpool's Source Assurance Program has been quite effective in reducing inspection costs and quality control problems in production. A further bonus of the program is the new spirit of cooperation that prevails between Whirlpool and its vendors. Animosity between supplier and buyer seems to be dwindling as Whirlpool's vendors realize they will be rewarded with steady business if they live up to their part of the bargain.

Quality circles at the Findlay plant have also contributed considerably to the J-I-T program. Five circles made up of six to ten employees from the same department meet on a regular basis to solve problems they encounter in their work areas. What keeps the circles going is the employees' sense of involvement in their company's progress—they know that their efforts play an important role. Whirlpool has found that the employees have been most receptive to the changes and are committed to making J-I-T work.

CHRYSLER CORPORATION

At the Chrysler Corporation's new Sterling Heights, Michigan, assembly plant for the LeBaron GTS and Dodge Lancer, roughly 70 percent of the parts are supplied on a just-in-time basis, mostly from firms located within 400 miles of the plant. Where carrying several days' worth of parts was once the norm, Chrysler has now cut most inventories to enough for just a few hours.

Chrysler has gone the just-in-time route by way of a new four-way program that has engineered improvements in containerization, dock operations, in-plant transportation, and line-feeding methods. Dan Keenan, corporate manager of materials handling engineering at Chrysler, had this to say in a *Modern Materials Handling* article:

> Our four-way program for streamlining just-in-time parts input maintains parts quality at the Sterling Heights Plant. And it will ultimately save $10 million a year by eliminating 6,500 tons of waste packaging material, including 400,000 expendable wooden pallets. It also minimizes freight and handling costs, and makes parts readily accessible to workers at the production line.[13]

Controlling parts input helps make the program tick. The LeBaron GTS and Dodge Lancers are manufactured on build schedules based on firm customer orders, whereby they are locked into an exact build sequence from the time they enter assembly until they come off the conveyor. All material requirements are therefore known in advance—a great aid in planning for just-in-time parts procurement. Suppliers to the Sterling Heights plant are given a day-by-day and hour-by-hour schedule of the parts that are needed at the production line up to seven days in advance.

Keenan describes how materials are monitored at the plant:

> A sophisticated computer tracking system, which includes the parts suppliers, keeps tabs on the quantity, quality, and location of all parts. Performance feedback utilizes 1,000 production data terminals at work stations, and 33 strategically located CRTs and graphic displays that monitor activity.[14]

Chrysler has established a 54-inch height limit for stock at the line, except in the case of large parts or other special requirements. This controls against the buildup of inventory, and the company maintains that it also improves working conditions and facilitates communication between the assembly workers and their supervisors.

At Chrysler, just-in-time manufacturing is not merely a means of reducing the inventory of parts, assemblies, and final products. It's a system that attempts to eliminate waste in every form. The old paper or wooden packaging materials, which included corrugated containers, disposable pallets, and combustible interior packaging materials, caused housekeeping problems and fire hazards. They've been replaced by various sorts of returnable, stackable, adjustable, and collapsible steel and plastic containers that have much longer service lives and require low maintenance. Container sizes have been engineered to optimize parts density and cube utilization in full trailers. Stackable containers have been designed to fit the inside height of trailers. Adjustable containers have been created to hold different parts. And new containers may be collapsed when emptied and stacked for returns from the plant. Highway trailers can often simultaneously carry as many of these collapsible containers as they can carry full ones, reducing the unit freight cost and frequency of returns.

Chrysler now relies on highway shipments for most supplies, rather than railroad cars, and they have improved dock operations to accommodate frequent, closely timed deliveries. Dock areas for incoming parts are strategically located close to the point of use. Dedicated docks have been set up to deliver underbody floor pans, parts for the body shop, paint supplies, tires and wheels, auto seats, parts for the trim, chassis, and final assembly lines, and engines to the areas where they will be used in production. Parts and assemblies no longer have to wait at a central dock.

With these new docks, internal transportation routes are shorter. Automatic guided vehicles are used throughout the plant to move thousands of small-parts container loads the short distances from the dock area to stations at the trim, chassis, and final assembly lines. Statistical data on the vehicles' activities are maintained by a central computer system.

Parts are made accessible to production workers by way of gravity-flow systems, consisting of upper and lower gravity-flow sections, which transport full rackloads of underbody floor pans, door assemblies, hoods, fenders, engines, and other parts to the work stations. Full racks are placed onto the upper level by fork trucks and moved forward by gravity toward a hydraulic lift platform. Each rackload of parts moves when needed to the lower level for removal by the workers. Once emptied, containers are released into the inclined lower level and removed by a fork truck to be returned to the supplier.

NOTES

1. Dave Pinch, "Corporate-Wide Implementation of ZIPS at Omark Industries (Zero Inventory Production System)," (Address given in Portland, Oregon, n.d.), 3.

2. Michael J. Rowney, "Early Experiences with ZIPS (Zero Inventory Production System) at Omark," Unpublished, n.d., 2.

3. Shigeo Shingo, *Study of Toyota Production System from Industrial Engineering Viewpoint* (Tokyo: Japanese Management Association, 1981).

4. "Short Term Inventory Reduction," *Just-in-Time*, no. 1, April 1, 1985, 2.

5. "JIT at Capacitor Products," *Just-in-Time*, no. 1, April 1, 1985, 2.

6. "Lessons Learned by JIT Implementers in G.E.," *Just-in-Time*, no. 1, April 1, 1985, 2.

7. Xerox Computer Services, "Just-in-Time Manufacturing Survival Kit" (Los Angeles: Xerox Corporation, 1986).

8. Ibid., sec. 2, p. 2.

9. Ibid.

10. Ibid., sec. 2, p. 3.

11. Ibid.

12. The five procedures are adapted from ibid., sec. 3, pp. 1–2.

13. Robert Jacobs and Vincent A. Mabert, eds., *Production Planning, Scheduling, and Inventory Control: Concepts, Techniques, and Systems,* 3d ed. (Engineering and Management Press, the Institute of Industrial Engineers, 1986), 261.

14. Ibid.

THE QUALITY CONTROL PROCESS

6 STATISTICAL QUALITY CONTROL

The need for formal quality standards has existed in American industry since mass production began during the industrial revolution. Large variations in the products that were manufactured became a pressing concern for those attempting to produce on a mass scale. By the time the First World War erupted, mass production was well established, but the lack of industrywide standardization made it almost impossible to mate parts from different manufacturers.

Statistical quality control techniques started to evolve during the 1920s, when Walter Shewhart of Bell Labs developed control charts to identify the causes of variation in a manufacturing process. His work would be of tremendous value to industry, but had no immediate impact for economic reasons. During the Depression, industry did not have the financial resources to invest in quality control. Despite this, by the time World War II broke out, some progress had already been made. Mobilized efforts to produce goods for the war greatly stimulated the development of standards and the use of quality control methods.

Once the war was over, quality control no longer seemed as essential. The average American, hungry for the good life, finally had the means to purchase it. American industry never had it so good—foreign competition was nil, demand was keener than ever, and the American manufacturer just couldn't produce fast enough to satisfy the whims of his customers. And as long as everything produced was quickly consumed, why should any firm worry about quality control? American manufacturers certainly didn't. All they were concerned about was how to speed up production.

Meanwhile, Japanese industrialists were earnestly studying how to overcome their pre-war reputation of being producers for the junkman. Prior to World War II, Japanese goods usually were of very poor quality. However, in an attempt to deceive the American buyer into believing he was purchasing a quality American product, some Japanese goods were stamped "Made in USA." In reality, what the American buyer was purchasing was a low quality product manufactured in USA, Japan.

In 1950, American statistician W. Edwards Deming embarked on a campaign to impart his knowledge of quality control concepts and methodology. During his meetings with top managers in Japanese industry, Deming laid down several principles to improve quality and productivity. He emphasized the importance of top management's role in promoting quality and consistently striving to better their companies' product or service. He also stressed the necessity of building in quality by improving the process rather than relying on mass inspection, which he repeatedly affirmed was nothing more than a waste of time and money. Only when statistical evidence indicates that the process is under control will quality products be manufactured. Improving the manufacturing process requires management to institute modern methods of on-the-job training. Employees must be well-schooled in statistical methods in order to identify the causes of variation within the manufacturing process and take the necessary corrective action. No employee should be afraid to ask questions, seek clarification of instructions, or report on poor working conditions. Fear should be completely driven out.

Deming also firmly believed that purchasing managers should cease to award business to vendors on the basis of price alone. Those suppliers who can provide statistical evidence of quality should be retained on a long-term basis to assure a continuous inflow of quality parts. Those who cannot should be dropped.

Organizational structures need to be modified to encourage communication between departments. "Break down barriers between staff areas" is Deming's recommendation. Problems with materials and specifications frequently arise when units work in isolation. When research, design, engineering, sales, and production work together as a team to produce the final output, such problems may be resolved before a major crisis occurs.

Numerical quotas don't fit in with Deming's theory of quality management. In his view, quota systems guarantee inefficiency. Far too often, employees will rush to meet their quotas without regard to quality. Moreover, quotas place a ceiling on production, abolish teamwork, and encourage rivalry and politicking.

Employees, at all levels, should take pride in their work. Assembly-line workers can produce quality, but not with poorly maintained machinery, poor training, and poor management. With proper guidance and the necessary tools, any work force anywhere in the world can manufacture a high-quality product.

Prior to World War II, the Ford Motor Company implemented a statistical process control system. Although the system fell into disuse during the post-War period of frenzied production, today production workers at the Ford Motor Company receive extensive training in the fundamentals of statistical quality control. The following text and illustrations, which describe the basics of statistical process control, are exerpted from Ford Motor Company's 1984 booklet, *Continuing Process Control and Process Capability Improvement.*

Figure 6-1. A Process Control System.

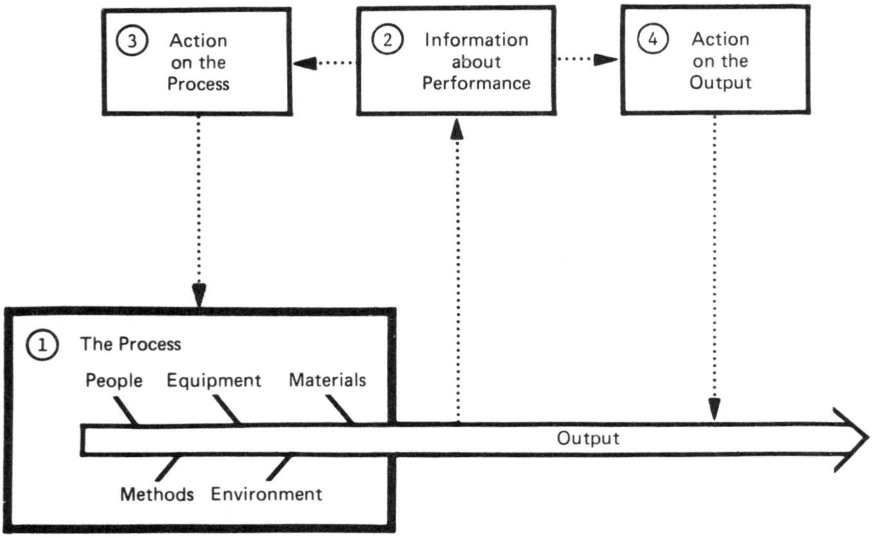

FUNDAMENTALS OF STATISTICAL PROCESS CONTROL

A Process Control System

A process control system can be described as a feedback system consisting of the following four elements:

1. The Process—By the process, we mean the whole combination of people, equipment, input materials, methods, and environment that work together to produce output. The total performance of the process—the quality of its output and its productive efficiency—depends on the way the process has been designed and

Ford Motor Company, *Continuing Process Control and Process Capability Improvement: A Guide to the Use of Control Charts for Improving Quality and Productivity for Company, Supplier and Dealer Activities* (Dearborn, Michigan, 1984). Should the reader have any questions about this manual, they should be addressed to P.T. Jessup, Statistical Methods Associate, Statistical Methods Office, Operations Support Staffs, Ford Motor Company, Room 524, WHO, P.O. Box 1899, Dearborn, Michigan 48121-1899.

built, and on the way it is operated. The rest of the process control system is useful only if it contributes to improved performance of the process.

2. Information About Performance—Much information about the actual performance of the process can be learned by studying the process output. In a broad sense, process output includes not only the products that are produced, but also any intermediate "outputs" that describe the operating state of the process, such as temperatures, cycle times, etc. If this information is gathered and interpreted correctly, it can show whether action is necessary to correct the process or the just-produced output. If timely and appropriate actions are not taken, however, any information-gathering effort is wasted.

3. Action on the Process—Action on the process is *future-oriented*, as it is taken when necessary to *prevent* the production of out-of-specification products. This action might consist of changes in the operations (e.g., operator training, changes to the incoming materials, etc.) or the more basic elements of the process itself (e.g., the equipment—which may need rehabilitation, or the design of the process as a whole—which may be vulnerable to changes in shop temperature or humidity). The effect of actions should be monitored, and further analysis and action should be taken if necessary.

4. Action on the Output—Action on the output is *past-oriented*, because it involves *detecting* out-of-specification output already produced. Unfortunately, if current output does not consistently meet customer requirements, it may be necessary to sort all products and to scrap or rework any nonconforming items. This must continue until the necessary corrective action on the process has been taken and verified, or until the product specifications have been changed.

It is obvious that inspection followed by action only on the output is a poor substitute for effective first-time process performance. Therefore, the discussions that follow focus on gathering process information and analyzing it so that action can be taken to correct the process itself.

Figure 6–2. Variation: Common and Special Causes.

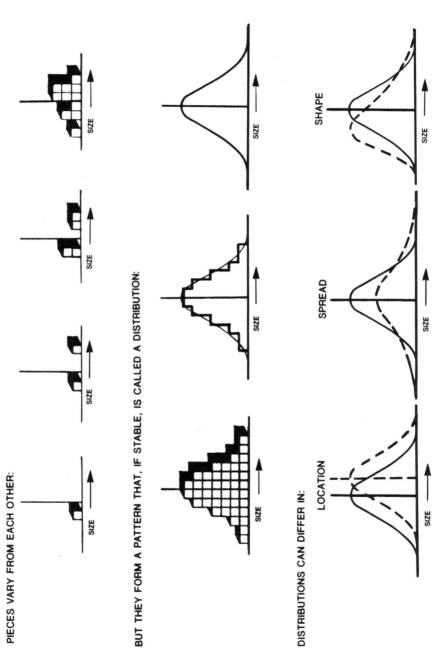

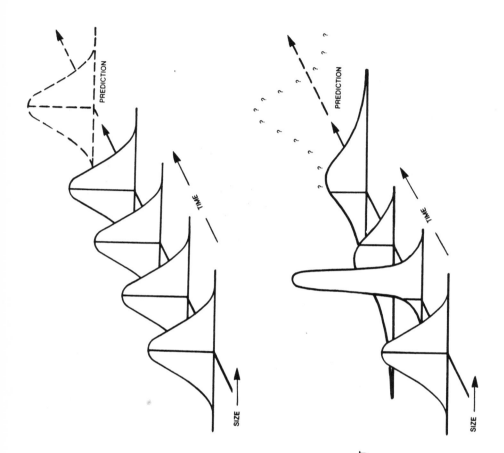

IF ONLY COMMON CAUSES OF VARI-
ATION ARE PRESENT, THE OUTPUT
OF A PROCESS FORMS A DISTRIBU-
TION THAT IS STABLE OVER TIME
AND IS PREDICTABLE:

IF SPECIAL CAUSES OF VARIATION
ARE PRESENT, THE PROCESS OUTPUT
IS NOT STABLE OVER TIME AND IS
NOT PREDICTABLE:

Variation: Common and Special Causes

In order to effectively use process control measurement data, it is important to understand the concept of variation. No two products or characteristics are exactly alike, because any process contains many sources of variability. The differences among products may be large, or they may be almost unmeasurably small, but they are always present. The diameter of a machined shaft, for instance, would be susceptible to potential variation from the machine (clearances, bearing wear), tool (strength, rate of wear), material (diameter, hardness), operator (part feed, accuracy of centering), maintenance (lubrication, replacement of worn parts), and environment (temperature, constancy of power supply). For another example, the time required to process an invoice could vary according to the people performing various steps, the reliability of any equipment they were using, the accuracy and legibility of the invoice itself, the procedures followed, and the volume of other work in the office.

Some sources of variation in the process cause very short-run piece-to-piece differences—e.g., backlash and clearances within a machine and its fixturing, or the accuracy of a bookkeeper's work. Other sources of variation tend to cause changes in the output only over a longer period of time, either gradually as with tool or machine wear, step-wise as with procedural changes, or irregularly, as with environmental changes such as power surges. Therefore, the time period and conditions over which measurements are made will affect the amount of the total variation that will be present.

From the standpoint of minimum requirements, the issue of variation is often simplified: parts within specification tolerances are acceptable, parts beyond specification tolerances are not acceptable; reports on time are acceptable, late reports are not acceptable. However, to manage any process and reduce variation, the variation must be traced back to its sources. The first step is to make the distinction between common and special causes of variation.

Common causes refer to the many sources of variation within a process that is in statistical control. They behave like a constant system of chance causes. While individual measured values are all different, as a group they tend to form a pattern that can be described as a distribution. This distribution can be characterized by:

- Location (typical value)
- Spread (amount by which the smaller values differ from the larger ones)
- Shape (the pattern of variation—whether it is symmetrical, peaked, etc.)

Special causes (often called assignable causes) refer to any factors causing variation that cannot be adequately explained by any single distribution of the process output, as would be the case if the process were in statistical control. Unless all the special causes of variation are identified and corrected, they will continue to affect the process output in unpredictable ways.

Local Actions and Actions on the System

There is an important connection between the two types of variation just discussed and the types of action necessary to reduce them.

Special Causes of variation can be detected by simple statistical techniques. These causes of variation are not common to all the operations involved. The discovery of a special cause of variation, and its removal, are usually the responsibility of someone who is directly connected with the operation, although management sometimes is in a better position to correct it. The resolution of a special cause of variation, then, usually requires *local action.*

The extent of *Common Causes* of variation can be indicated by simple statistical techniques, but the causes themselves need more detailed analysis to isolate. These common causes of variation are usually the responsibility of management to correct, although other people directly connected with the operation sometimes are in a better position to identify these causes and pass them on to management for correction. Overall, though, the resolution of common causes of variation usually requires *actions on the system.*

Only a relatively small proportion of all process troubles—industrial experience suggests about 15%—is correctable locally by people directly connected with the operation; the majority—the other 85%—is correctable only by management action on the system. Confusion about the type of action to take is very costly to the organization, in terms of wasted effort, delayed resolution of trouble, and aggravated problems. It would be wrong, for example, to take local action (e.g., adjusting a machine) when management action on the system was required (e.g., selecting suppliers that provide consistent input materials).

Process Capability and Process Control

The goal of a process control system is to make economically sound decisions about actions affecting the process. This means balancing the risks of taking action when action is not necessary (overcontrol) versus failing to take action when action is necessary (undercontrol). These risks must be handled, however, in the context of the two sources of variation previously mentioned—special causes and common causes.

A process is said to be operating in statistical control when the only source of variation is common causes. "But a state of statistical control is not a natural state for a manufacturing process. It is instead an achievement, arrived at by elimination, one by one, by determined effort, of special causes of excessive variation" (W. Edwards Deming, "On Some Statistical Aids Toward Economic Production," *Interfaces* 5, no. 4 (August 1975): 5]. The initial function of a process control system, then, is to provide a statistical signal when special causes of variation are present, and to avoid giving false signals when they are not present. This will enable appropriate action that can eliminate those special causes and prevent their reappearance.

Process capability is determined by the total variation that comes from common causes—the minimum variation that can be achieved after all special causes have been eliminated. Thus capability represents the performance of the process itself, as demonstrated when the process is being operated in a state of statistical control. Capability is often thought of in terms of the proportion of output that will be within product specification tolerances. Since a process in statistical control can be described by a predictable distribution, the proportion of out-of-specification parts can be estimated from this distribution. As long as the process remains in statistical control, it will continue to produce the same proportion of out-of-specification parts. Management actions to reduce the variation from common causes are required to improve the process' ability to meet specifications consistently.

Figure 6-3.   Process Control and Process Capability.

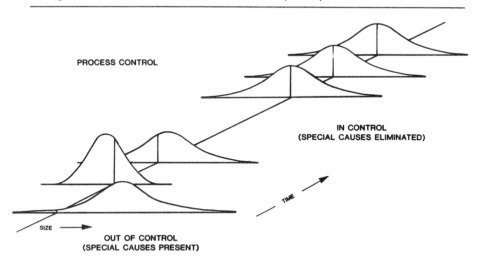

PROCESS CONTROL

IN CONTROL
(SPECIAL CAUSES ELIMINATED)

TIME

SIZE

OUT OF CONTROL
(SPECIAL CAUSES PRESENT)

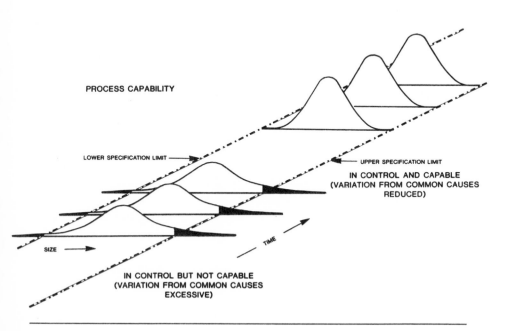

PROCESS CAPABILITY

LOWER SPECIFICATION LIMIT

UPPER SPECIFICATION LIMIT

IN CONTROL AND CAPABLE
(VARIATION FROM COMMON CAUSES
REDUCED)

SIZE

TIME

IN CONTROL BUT NOT CAPABLE
(VARIATION FROM COMMON CAUSES
EXCESSIVE)

In short: the process must first be brought into statistical control by detecting and eliminating special causes of variation. Then its performance is predictable, and its capability to meet customer expectations can be assessed. This is the basis for continuing improvement.

Control Charts: Tools for Process Control

Dr. Walter Shewhart of the Bell Laboratories, while studying process data in the 1920s, first made the distinction between controlled and uncontrolled variation, due to what we call common and special causes. He developed a simple but powerful tool to dynamically separate the two—the control chart. Since that time, control charts have been used successfully in a wide variety of process-control situations, both in the U.S. and other countries, notably Japan. Experience has shown that control charts effectively direct attention toward special causes of variation when they appear and reflect the extent of common cause variation that must be reduced by management action.

Several types of control charts have been developed, to analyze both variables and attributes. However, all control charts have the same two basic uses. Using Shewhart's terms, they are:

- As a judgment, to give evidence whether a process has been operating in a state of statistical control, and to signal the presence of special causes of variation so that corrective action can be taken.

- As an operation, to maintain the state of statistical control limits as a basis for real-time decisions.

Process improvement using control charts is an iterative procedure, repeating the fundamental phases of collection, control, and capability. First, data are gathered according to a careful plan, then, these data are used to calculate control limits, which are the basis of interpreting the data for statistical control. When the process is in statistical control, it can be interpreted for process capability. To monitor improvements in control and capability, the cycle begins again, as more data are gathered, interpreted, and used as the basis for action.

1. Collection: The process is run, and data for the characteristic being studied are gathered and converted to a form that can be

Figure 6-4. Control Charts.

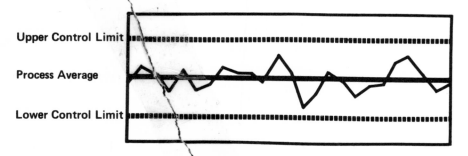

Upper Control Limit

Process Average

Lower Control Limit

1. *Collection*:
   - Gather data and plot on a chart.

2. *Control*:
   - Calculate control limits from process data, using simple formulas.
   - Identify special causes of variation; take local actions to correct.

3. *Capability*:
   - Quantify common cause variation; take action on the system.

These three phases are repeated for continuing process improvement.

---

plotted on a graph. These data might be the measured values of a dimension of a machined piece, the number of flaws in a bolt of vinyl, railcar transit times, number of bookkeeping errors, etc.

2. Control: Trial control limits are calculated based upon data from the output of the process; they reflect the amount of variation that could be expected if only variation from common causes was present. They are drawn on the chart as a guide to analysis. Control limits are not specification limits or objectives, but are reflections of the natural variability of the process.

The data are then compared with the control limits to see whether the variation is stable and appears to come only from common causes. If special causes of variation are evident, operation of the process is studied to determine what is affecting the process. After actions (usually local) have been taken, further data are collected, control limits are recalculated if necessary, and any additional special causes are studied and corrected.

3. Capability: After all special causes have been corrected and the process is running in statistical control, the process capability can be assessed. If the variation from common causes is excessive, the process cannot produce output that consistently meets customer needs. The process itself must be investigated, and management action must be taken to improve the system.

For continuing process improvement, repeat these three phases. Gather more data as appropriate; work to reduce process variation by operating the process in statistical control and continually improving its capability.

Benefits of Control Charts

The following list summarizes the benefits that can come from using control charts. It includes items from the experience of writers in this field, such as Dr. Deming, and our own experience within Ford:

- Control charts are simple and effective tools to achieve statistical control. They lend themselves to being maintained at the job station by the operator. They give the people closest to the operation reliable information on when action should be taken—and on when action should *not* be taken.

- When a process is in statistical control, its performance to specification will be predictable. Thus, both producer and customer can rely on consistent quality levels, and both can rely on stable costs of achieving that quality level.

- After a process is in statistical control, its performance can be further improved to reduce variation. The expected effects of proposed improvements in the system can be anticipated, and the actual effects of even relatively subtle changes can be identified through the control chart data. Such process improvements will:

  - Increase the percentage of output that meets customer expectations (improve quality),
  - Decrease the output requiring scrap or rework (improve cost per good unit produced), and

—Increase the total yield of acceptable output through the process (improve effective capacity).

● Control charts provide a common language for communications about the performance of a process—between the two or three shifts that operate a process; between line production (operator, supervisor) and support activities (maintenance, material control, process engineering, quality control); between different stations in the process; between supplier and user; between the manufacturing/assembly plant and the design engineering activity.

● Control charts, by distinguishing special from common causes of variation, give a good indication of whether any problems are likely to be correctable locally or will require management action. This minimizes the confusion, frustration, and excessive cost of misdirected problem-solving efforts.

CONTROL CHARTS FOR VARIABLES

Control charts for variables are powerful tools that can be used when measurements from a process are available. Examples would be the diameter of a bearing, the closing effort of a door, or the time to review a voucher. Variables charts—and especially their most common forms, the $\overline{X}$ (X bar) and R charts—represent the classic application of control charting to process control.

Control charts for variables are particularly useful for several reasons:

1. Most processes and their outputs have characteristics that are measurable, so the potential applicability is broad.

2. A measurement value (e.g., "the diameter is 16.45 mm") contains more information than a simple yes-no statement (e.g., "the diameter is within specification").

3. Although obtaining one piece of measured data is generally more costly than obtaining one piece of go/no-go data, fewer pieces need be checked to get more information about the process, so in some cases total inspection costs can be lower.

4. Because fewer pieces need to be checked before making reliable decisions, the time gap between production of parts and corrective action can be shortened.

5. With variables data, performance of a process can be analyzed even if all individual values are within the specification limits; this is important in seeking never-ending improvement.

Variables charts can explain processes data in terms of both its spread (piece-to-piece variability) and its location (process average). Thus, control charts for variables are almost always prepared and analyzed in pairs—one chart for location and another for spread. The most commonly used pair are the $\overline{X}$ and R charts which will be discussed here in detail. $\overline{X}$ is the average of the values in small subgroups—a measure of location; R is the range of values within each subgroup (highest minus lowest)—a measure of spread.

$\overline{X}$ and R Charts

Before $\overline{X}$ and R charts can be used, several preparatory steps must be taken:

- Establish an environment suitable for action. Any statistical method will fail unless management has prepared a responsive environment. Fear within the organization that inhibits people from being candid must be removed. People who do not know their job must be trained. People must be evaluated on quality, not just quantity. Management must provide resources to support improvement actions.

- Define the process. The process must be understood in terms of its relationship to other operations/users both upstream and downstream, and in terms of the process elements (people, equipment, materials, methods and environment) that affect it at each stage. Techniques such as the cause-and-effect diagram help make these relationships visible and allow the pooling of experience from people who understand different aspects of the process.

- Determine characteristics to be managed. Study efforts should be concentrated on those characteristics that are most promising for process improvement (an application of the Pareto principle). Several considerations are appropriate:

  - The customer's needs. This includes both any subsequent processes that use the product or service as an input, and the final end-item customer. Communication of the needs of both types of customer to the point in the process where improvement can occur takes teamwork and understanding.

—Current and potential problem areas. Consider existing evidence of waste or poor performance (e.g., scrap, rework, excessive overtime, missed targets) and areas of risk (e.g., upcoming changes to the design of the product or service, or to any elements of the process). These are opportunities for improvement, requiring application of all the disciplines involved in running the business.

—Correlation between characteristics. For an efficient and effective study, take advantage of relationships among characteristics. For instance, if the characteristic of concern is difficult to measure (e.g., volume), track a correlated characteristic that is easier to measure (e.g., weight). Also, if several individual characteristics on an end item tend to vary together, it may be sufficient to chart only one of them.

• Define the measurement system. The characteristic must be operationally defined, so that findings can be communicated to all concerned in ways that have the same meaning today as yesterday. This involves specifying what information is to be gathered, where, how, and under what conditions. The measurement equipment itself must be predictable for both accuracy and precision— periodic calibration is not enough.

• Minimize unnecessary variation. Unnecessary external causes of variation should be reduced before the study begins. This could simply mean watching that the process is being operated as intended, or it could mean conducting a controlled study with known input materials, constant control settings, etc. The purpose is to avoid obvious problems that could and should be corrected even without use of control charts; this includes excessive process adjustment or overcontrol. In all cases, a process log should be kept noting all relevant events such as tool changes, new raw material lots, etc. This will aid in subsequent problem analysis.

Step 1: Gather Data

An $\overline{X}$ and an R chart, as a pair, are developed from measurements of a particular characteristic of the process output. These data are reported in small subgroups of constant size, usually including from 2 to 5 consecutive pieces, with subgroups taken periodically (e.g., once every 15 minutes, twice per shift, etc.). A data gathering plan must be developed and used as the basis for collecting, recording and plotting the data on a chart.

1.a. Select the Size, Frequency, and Number of Subgroups

• Subgroup Size—The subgroups should be chosen so that opportunities for variation among the units within a subgroup are small. If the variation within a subgroup represents the piece-to-piece variability over a very short period of time, then any unusual variation between subgroups would reflect changes in the process that should be investigated for appropriate action.

For an initial study of a process, the subgroups could typically consist of 4 to 5 consecutively-produced pieces representing only a single tool, head, die cavity, etc. (i.e., a single process stream). The intention is that the pieces within each subgroup would all be produced under very similar production conditions over a very short time interval with no other systematic relationship to each other; hence, variation within each subgroup would primarily reflect common causes.

• Subgroup Frequency—Subgroups should be collected often enough, and at appropriate times, so that they can reflect the potential opportunities for change. Such potential causes of change could be shift patterns or relief operators, warmup trend, material lots, etc.

• Number of Subgroups—The number of subgroups should satisfy two criteria. From a process standpoint, enough subgroups should be gathered to assure that the major sources of variation have had an opportunity to appear. From a statistical standpoint, 25 or more subgroups containing about 100 or more individual readings give a good test for stability and, if stable, good estimates of the process location and spread.

In some cases, existing data may be available which could accelerate this first phase of the study. However, they should be used only if they are recent and if the basis for establishing subgroups is clearly understood.

1.b. Set Up Control Charts and Record Raw Data

$\overline{X}$ and R charts are normally drawn with the $\overline{X}$ chart above the R chart, and a data block at the bottom. The values of $\overline{X}$ and R will be the vertical scales, while the sequence of subgroups through time will be the horizontal scale. The data values and the plot points for the range and average should be aligned vertically.

The data block should include space for each of the individual readings. It should also include a space for the sum of the readings, the average ($\overline{X}$), the range (R), and the date/time or other identification of the subgroup.

Enter the individual raw values and the identification for each subgroup.

1.c. Calculate the Average ($\overline{X}$) and Range (R) of Each Subgroup

The characteristics to be plotted are the sample average ($\overline{X}$) and the sample range (R) for each subgroup; these reflect the overall process average and its variability, respectively.

For each subgroup, calculate:

$$\overline{X} = \frac{X_1 + X_2 + \ldots + X_n}{n}$$

$$R = X_{highest} - X_{lowest}$$

where the X_1, X_2 ... are individual values within the subgroup and n is the subgroup sample size.

1.d. Select Scales for the Control Charts

The vertical scales for the two charts are for measured values of $\overline{X}$ and R respectively. Some general guidelines for determining the scales may be helpful, although they may have to be modified in particular circumstances. For the $\overline{X}$ chart, the difference between the highest and lowest values on the scale should be at least 2 times the difference between the highest and lowest subgroup averages ($\overline{X}$). For the R chart, values should extend from a lower value of zero to an upper value about 2 times the largest range (R) encountered during the initial period.

Note: One helpful guide is to set the scale spacing for the range chart to be double that of the averages chart (e.g., if 1

Figure 6-5.   Recording Data on the Control Chart.

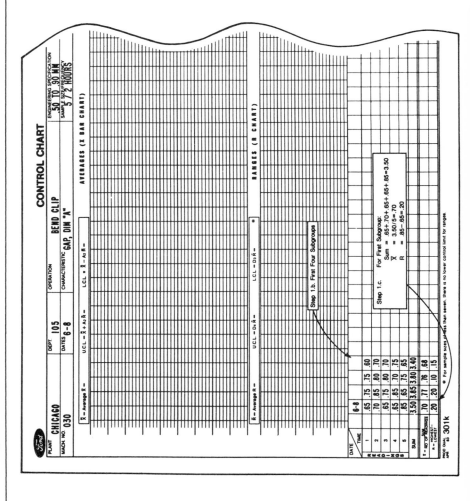

Figure 6-6. Plotting the Data on the Control Chart.

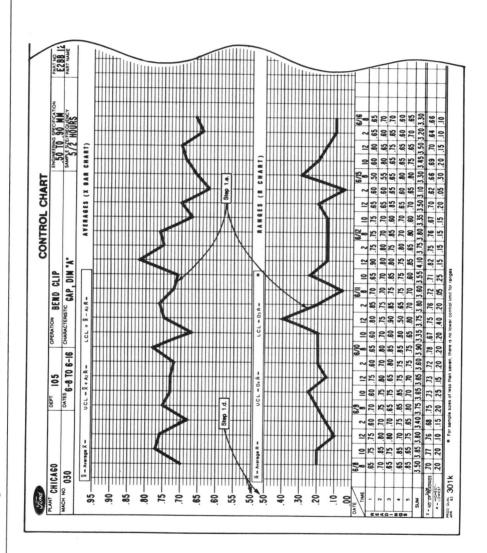

scale unit equals .01 inches on the averages chart, 1 scale unit would equal .02 inches on the range chart). For typical subgroup sizes, the control limits for averages and ranges will be about the same width, a visual aid to analysis.

1.e. Plot the Averages and Ranges on the Control Charts

Plot the averages and ranges on their respective charts. Connect the points with lines to help visualize patterns and trends.

Briefly scan the plot points to see if they look reasonable; if any points are substantially higher or lower than the others, confirm that the calculations and plots are correct. Make sure that the plot points for the corresponding $\overline{X}$ and R are vertically in line.

Step 2. Calculate Control Limits

Control limits for the range chart are developed first, then those for the chart for averages. The calculations for the control limits for variables charts use constants, which appear as letters in the formulas that follow. These factors, which differ according to the subgroup size (n), are shown for illustrative purposes in brief tables accompanying the respective formulas. Complete tables may be found in the American Society for Testing and Materials publication, *Manual on the Presentation of Data and Control Chart Analysis* [STP-15D (Philadelphia: American Society for Testing and Materials, 1976)].

2.a. Calculate the average Range ($\overline{R}$) and the Process Average ($\overline{\overline{X}}$)

For the study period, calculate:

$$\overline{R} = \frac{R_1 + R_2 + \ldots + R_k}{k}$$

$$\overline{\overline{X}} = \frac{\overline{X}_1 + \overline{X}_2 + \ldots + \overline{X}_k}{k}$$

where k is the number of subgroups, R_1 and $\overline{X}_1$ are the range and average of the first subgroup, R_2 and $\overline{X}_2$ are from the second subgroup, etc.

2.b. Calculate the Control Limits

Control limits are then calculated to show the extent by which the subgroup averages and ranges would vary if only common causes of variation were present. They are based on the sub-group sample size and the amount of within-subgroup variability reflected in the ranges. Calculate the upper and lower control limits for ranges and for averages:

$$UCL_R = D_4 \overline{R}$$

$$LCL_R = D_3 \overline{R}$$

$$UCL_{\overline{x}} = \overline{\overline{X}} + A_2 \overline{R}$$

$$LCL_{\overline{x}} = \overline{\overline{X}} - A_2 \overline{R}$$

where D_4, D_3, and A_2 are constants varying by sample size. Values for sample sizes from 2 to 10 are shown in the following partial table:

n	2	3	4	5	6	7	8	9	10
D_4	3.27	2.57	2.28	2.11	2.00	1.92	1.86	1.82	1.78
D_3	*	*	*	*	*	.08	.14	.18	.22
A_2	1.88	1.02	.73	.58	.48	.42	.37	.34	.31

(for sample sizes below 7, the LCL_R would technically be a negative number; in those cases there is no lower control limit. This means that for a subgroup of size 6, six "identical" measurements would not be unreasonable).

2.c. Draw Lines for the Averages and the Control Limits on the Charts.

Draw the average range $(\overline{R})$ and process average $(\overline{\overline{X}})$ as solid horizontal lines, the control limits $(UCL_R, LCL_R, UCL_{\overline{x}}, LCL_{\overline{x}})$ as dashed horizontal lines; label the lines.

Step 3. Interpret for Process Control

The control limits can be interpreted as follows: If the process piece-to-piece variability and the process average were to remain constant at their present levels (as estimated by R and $\overline{X}$, respectively), the individual subgroup ranges (R) and averages $(\overline{X})$ would vary by chance alone, but they would seldom go beyond the control limits (less than 1% of the time for ranges, and only .27% of the time for averages, for the limits calculated above). Likewise, there would be no obvious trends or patterns in the data, beyond what would likely occur due to chance. The objective of control chart analysis is to

Figure 6–7. Determining the Average Range and the Process Average.

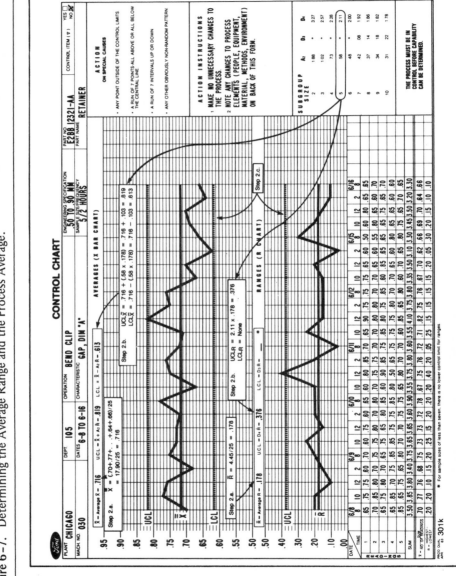

identify any evidence that the process variability or the process average are not operating at a constant level—that one or both are out of statistical control—and to take appropriate action.

3.a. Analyze the Data Plots on the Range Chart

1. Points Beyond the Control Limits—The presence of one or more points beyond either control limit on the range chart is primary evidence of non-control at that point. Since points beyond the control limits would be very rare if only variation from common causes were present, we presume that a special cause has accounted for the extreme value. Therefore, any point beyond a control limit is the signal for immediate analysis of the operation for the special cause.

Patterns or Trends Within the Control Limits—The presence of unusual patterns or trends, even when all ranges are within the control limits, can be evidence of noncontrol or change in process spread during the period of the pattern or trend. This could give the first warning of unfavorable conditions which should be corrected even before points are seen beyond the control limits. Conversely, certain patterns or trends could be favorable and should be studied for possible permanent improvement of the process.

2. The following are signs that a process shift or trend has begun:

Seven points in a row on one side of the average, or
Seven intervals in a row that are consistently increasing (equal to or greater than the preceding points) or consistently decreasing.

A run above the average range, or a run up signifies:

—Greater spread in the output values, which could be from an irregular cause (such as equipment malfunction) or from a shift in one of the process elements (e.g., a new, less uniform raw material lot). These are usually troubles that need correction.

—A change in the measurement system (e.g., new inspector or gage.

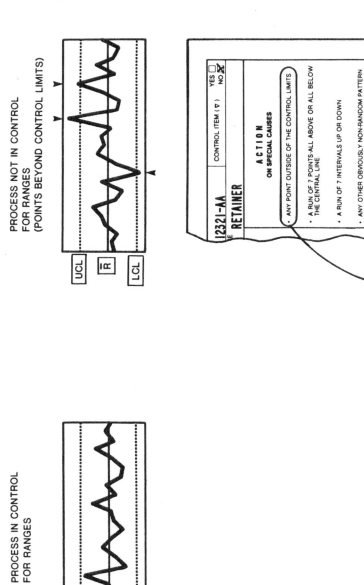

Figure 6-8. Analyzing the Range Chart: Any Point Outside of the Control Limits Signals Need for Action.

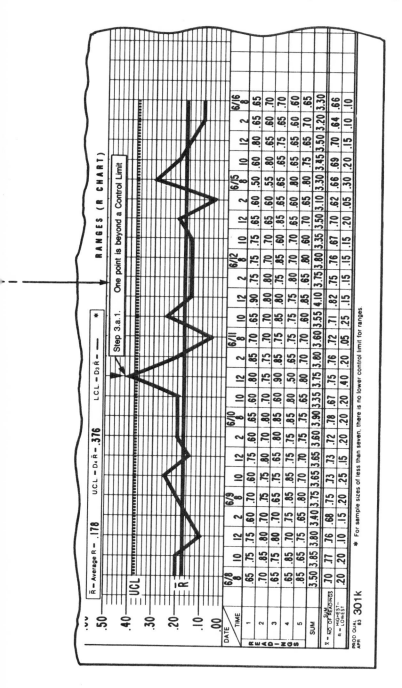

RANGES (R CHART)

R − Average R − .178   UCL − D₄R̄ − .376   LCL − D₃R̄ − *

Step 3.a.1.   One point is beyond a Control Limit

* For sample sizes of less than seven, there is no lower control limit for ranges.

PROD QUAL APR 63 301k

Figure 6-9. Analyzing the Range Chart: A Run of 7 Points Above or Below the Central Line or a Run of 7 Intervals Up or Down Signals Need for Action.

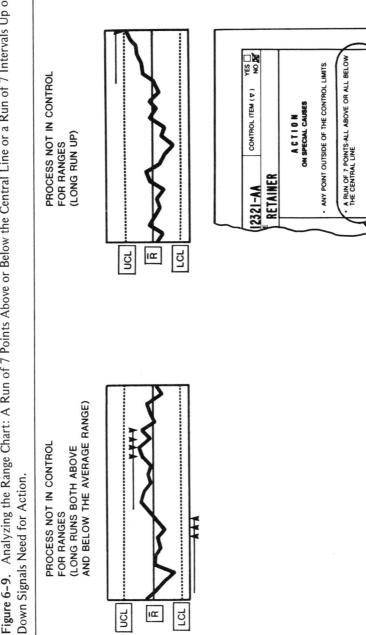

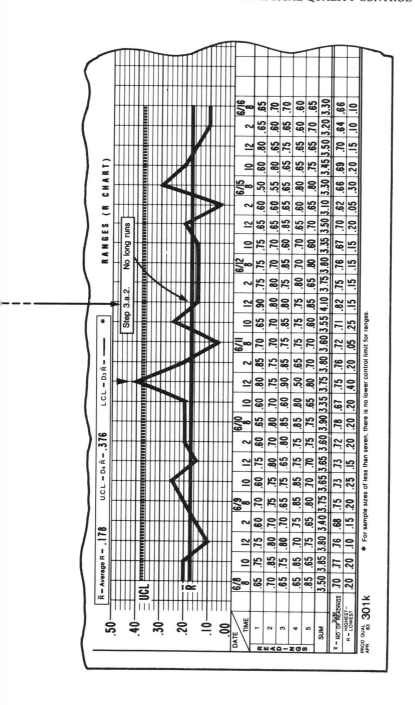

A run below the average range, or a run down signifies:

—Smaller spread in output values, which is usually a good condition that should be studied for wider application.
—A change in the measurement system, which could mask real performance changes.

3.b. Find and Correct Special Causes (Range Chart)

For each indication of a special cause in the range data, conduct an analysis of the operation of the process to determine the cause; correct that condition, and prevent it from recurring. The control chart itself should be a useful guide in problem analysis, suggesting when the condition began and how long it continued.

Timeliness is important in problem analysis, both in terms of minimizing the production of nonconforming output, and in terms of having fresh evidence for diagnosis. For instance, the appearance of a single point beyond the control limits is reason to begin an immediate analysis of the process.

It should be emphasized that problem-solving is often the most difficult and time-consuming step. Statistical input from the control chart can be an appropriate starting point, but other simple tools such as Pareto charts, cause-and-effect diagrams, or other graphical analysis can be helpful. Ultimately, however, the explanations for behavior lie within the process and the people who are involved with it. Thoroughness, patience, insight and understanding will be required to develop actions that will measurably improve performance.

3.c. Recalculate Control Limits (Range Chart)

When conducting an initial process study or a reassessment of process capability, the control limits should be recalculated to exclude the effects of out-of-control periods for which process causes have been found and corrected. Once all subgroups affected by the special causes have been corrected, new average range ($\overline{R}$) and control limits are calculated. It should be confirmed that all range points show control when compared to the new limits; if not, the identification/correction/recalculation sequence should be repeated.

Note: The exclusion of subgroups representing unstable conditions is not just "throwing away bad data." Rather, by excluding the points affected by known special causes, we have a better estimate of the background level of variation due to common causes. This, in turn, gives the most appropriate basis for the control limits used to detect future occurrences of special causes of variation.

3.d. Analyze the Data Plots on the Averages Chart

When the ranges in statistical control, the process spread—the within-subgroup variation—is considered to be stable. The averages can then be analyzed to see if the process location is changing over time. If the averages are in statistical control, they reflect only the amount of variation seen in the ranges—the common-cause variation of the system. If the averages are not in control, some special causes of variation are making the process location unstable.

1. Points Beyond the Control Limits—The presence of one or more points beyond either control limit is primary evidence of the presence of special causes at that point. It is the signal for immediate analysis of the operation. Mark such data points on the chart.

A point beyond either control limit is generally a sign that:

—The control limit or plot point are in error, or
—The process has shifted, either at that one point in time (possibly an isolated incident) or as part of a trend, or
—The measurement system has changes (e.g., different gage or inspector).

Patterns or Trends within the Control Limits—The presence of unusual patterns or trends can be evidence of non-control or change in capability during the period of the pattern or trend.

2. Runs—The following are signs that a process shift or trend has begun:

Seven points in a row on one side of the average, or
Seven intervals in a row that are consistently increasing or decreasing.

Figure 6–10.   Analyzing the Averages Chart: Any Point Outside of the Control Limits Signals Need for Action.

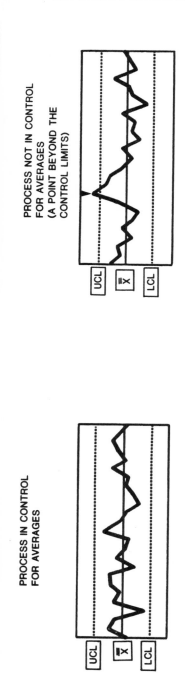

**PROCESS IN CONTROL
FOR AVERAGES**

UCL

$\overline{\overline{x}}$

LCL

**PROCESS NOT IN CONTROL
FOR AVERAGES
(A POINT BEYOND THE
CONTROL LIMITS)**

UCL

$\overline{\overline{x}}$

LCL

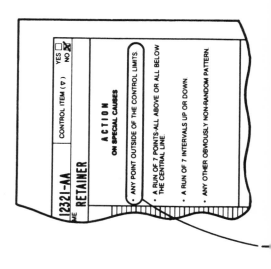

12321-AA   CONTROL ITEM (▽)   YES ☐
                                 NO ☒
ME RETAINER

**A C T I O N
ON SPECIAL CAUSES**

• ANY POINT OUTSIDE OF THE CONTROL LIMITS.

• A RUN OF 7 POINTS–ALL ABOVE OR ALL BELOW
  THE CENTRAL LINE.

• A RUN OF 7 INTERVALS UP OR DOWN.

• ANY OTHER OBVIOUSLY NON-RANDOM PATTERN.

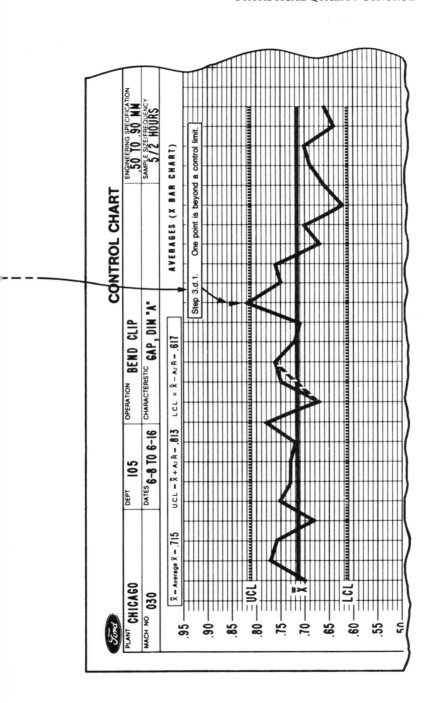

CONTROL CHART

PLANT **CHICAGO** DEPT. **105** OPERATION **BEND CLIP**

ENGINEERING SPECIFICATION **.50 TO .90 MM**

MACH NO. **030** DATES **6-8 TO 6-16** CHARACTERISTIC **GAP, DIM "A"**

SAMPLE SIZE/FREQUENCY **5/2 HOURS**

$\bar{X}$ = Average $\bar{X}$ = **.715**   UCL = $\bar{\bar{X}}$ + $A_2\bar{R}$ = **.813**   LCL = $\bar{\bar{X}}$ − $A_2\bar{R}$ = **.617**

AVERAGES (X BAR CHART)

Step 3.d.1.   One point is beyond a control limit.

.95
.90
.85
.80   UCL
.75
.70 $\bar{\bar{X}}$
.65
.60   LCL
.55
.50

Figure 6-11. Analyzing the Averages Chart: A Run of 7 Points Above or Below the Central Line or a Run of 7 Intervals Up or Down Signals Need for Action.

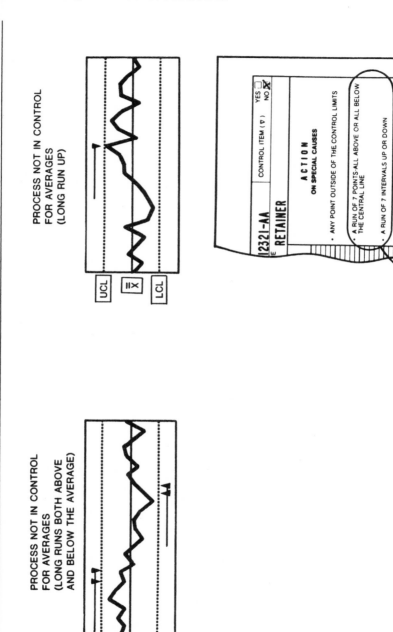

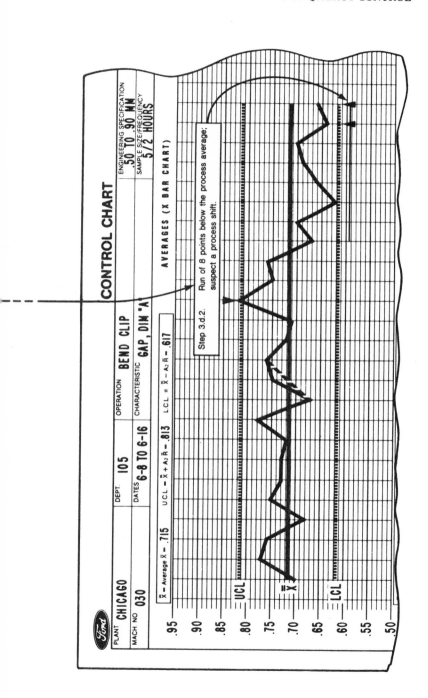

Figure 6-12.   Analyzing the Averages Chart: Any Obviously Non-Random Pattern Signals Need for Action.

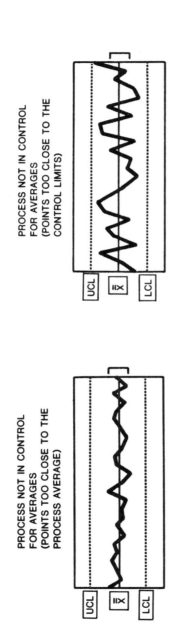

PROCESS NOT IN CONTROL
FOR AVERAGES
(POINTS TOO CLOSE TO THE
CONTROL LIMITS)

UCL
$\bar{\bar{x}}$
LCL

PROCESS NOT IN CONTROL
FOR AVERAGES
(POINTS TOO CLOSE TO THE
PROCESS AVERAGE)

UCL
$\bar{\bar{x}}$
LCL

12321-AA   CONTROL ITEM (▽)   YES ☐
                                  NO ☒

RETAINER

ACTION
ON SPECIAL CAUSES

• ANY POINT OUTSIDE OF THE CONTROL LIMITS

• A RUN OF 7 POINTS-ALL ABOVE OR ALL BELOW
  THE CENTRAL LINE.

• A RUN OF 7 INTERVALS UP OR DOWN

• ANY OTHER OBVIOUSLY NON-RANDOM PATTERN

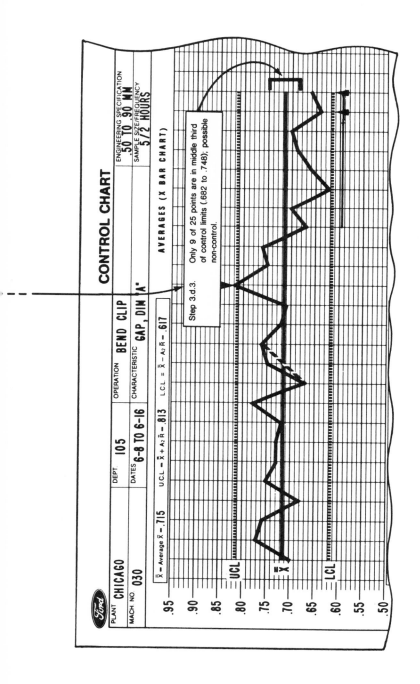

A run relative to the process average is generally a sign that:

— The process average has changed—and may still be changing, or
— The measurement system has changed.

3. Obvious Nonrandom Patterns—Other distinct patterns may also indicate the presence of special causes of variation, although care must be taken not to over-interpret the data. Among these patterns are trends, cycles, unusual spread of points within the control limits, and relationships among values within subgroups. One test for unusual spread is given below:

About 2/3 of the data points should lie within the middle third of the region between the control limits; about 1/3 of the points will be in the outer two-thirds of the region; and about 1/20 will lie relatively close to the control limits (in the outer third of the region).

3.e. Find and Correct Special Causes (Averages Chart)

For each indication of an out-of-control condition in the average data, conduct an analysis of the operation of the process to determine the reason for the special cause; correct that condition, and prevent it from recurring. Use the chart data as a guide to when problem conditions began and how long they continued. Timeliness in analysis is important, both for diagnosis and to minimize nonconforming output. Problem-solving techniques such as Pareto analysis and cause-and-effect analysis can help in the analysis.

3.f. Recalculate Control Limits (Averages Chart)

When conducting an initial process study or a reassessment of process capability, exclude any out-of-control points for which special causes have been found; recalculate and plot the process average and control limits. Confirm that all data points show control when compared to the new limits, repeating the identification/correction/recalculation sequence if necessary.

Step 4. Interpret for Process Capability

Having determined that a process is in statistical control, the question still remains whether the process is capable—i.e., does its output meet customer needs? To understand and improve the capability of a process, an important shift in thinking must occur: capability reflects variation from common causes, and management action on the system is almost always required for capability improvement.

Assessment of process capability begins after control issues in both the $\overline{X}$ and R charts have been resolved (special causes identified, analyzed, corrected and prevented from reoccurring), and the ongoing control charts reflect a process that is in statistical control, preferably for 25 or more subgroups. In general, the distribution of the process output is compared with the engineering specifications, to see whether these specifications can consistently be met.

There are many techniques for assessing the capability of a process that is in statistical control. Some assume that the process output follows the bell-shaped normal distribution. If it is not known whether the distribution is normal, a test for normality should be made such as reviewing a histogram, plotting on normal probability paper, or using more precise methods [e.g., those described in Acheson J. Duncan, *Quality Control and Industrial Statistics*, 4th ed. (Homewood, Ill., Richard D. Irwin, Inc., 1974)]. If nonnormality is suspected or confirmed, more flexible techniques should be used, such as computerized curve-fitting or graphical analysis. When the distribution shape is normal, the technique described below can be used. It involves only simple calculations based on data from the control chart. The process average $\overline{\overline{X}}$ is used as the location of the distribution. As a measure of spread, the standard deviation is used, estimated from a simple formula involving the average range $\overline{R}$.

4.a. Calculate the Process Standard Deviation

Since the within-subgroup process variability is reflected in the subgroup ranges, the estimate of the process standard deviation $\hat{\sigma}$ ("sigma hat") can be based on the average range $(\overline{R})$.

Calculate:

$$\hat{\sigma} = \overline{R}/d_2$$

where $\overline{R}$ is the average of the subgroup ranges (for periods with ranges in control) and d_2 is a constant varying by sample size, as shown in the partial table below:

n	2	3	4	5	6	7	8	9	10
d_2	1.13	1.69	2.06	2.33	2.53	2.70	2.85	2.97	3.08

Figure 6-13. Process Capability.

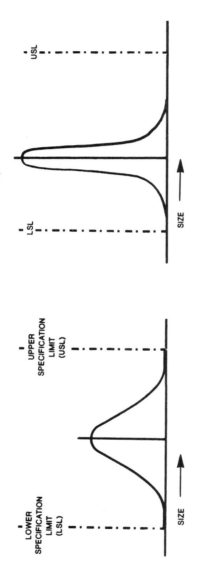

CAPABLE PROCESSES (VIRTUALLY ALL OUTPUT IS WITHIN THE SPECIFICATIONS):

NON-CAPABLE PROCESSES (OUTPUT IS PRODUCED BEYOND ONE OR BOTH SPECIFICATIONS):

STANDARD DEVIATION AND RANGE (FOR A GIVEN SAMPLE SIZE, THE LARGER THE AVERAGE RANGE
— $\bar{R}$, THE LARGER THE STANDARD DEVIATION — $\hat{\sigma}$):

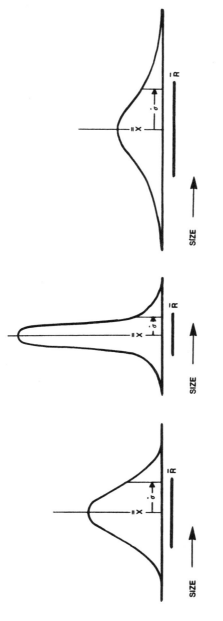

FROM THE EXAMPLE (ESTIMATING THE PROCESS STANDARD DEVIATION FROM THE AVERAGE RANGE):

$\bar{R}$ = .169
n = 5
d_2 = 2.33
$\hat{\sigma}$ = $\bar{R}/d_2$ = .169 / 2.33 = .0725

$\bar{\bar{X}}$ = .738
LSL = .500
USL = .900

This estimate of the process standard deviation ($\hat{\sigma}$) can be used in evaluating the process capability, as long as both the ranges and averages are in statistical control.

4.b. Calculate the Process Capability

Capability can be described in terms of the distance of the process average from the specification limits in standard deviation units, Z. Drawing a diagram that shows the distribution curve, X, the specification limits, and the Z values will be helpful.

- For a unilateral tolerance, calculate:

$$ Z = \frac{SL - \overline{\overline{X}}}{\hat{\sigma}} $$

where SL = specification limit, $\overline{\overline{X}}$ = measured process average, and $\hat{\sigma}$ = estimated process standard deviation.

- For bilateral tolerances, calculate:

$$ Z_{USL} = \frac{USL - \overline{\overline{X}}}{\hat{\sigma}} \qquad Z_{LSL} = \frac{LSL - \overline{\overline{X}}}{\hat{\sigma}} $$

$$ Z_{min} = \text{Minimum of } Z_{USL} \text{ or } -Z_{LSL} $$

where USL, LSL = upper and lower specification limits; a negative value of Z indicates a distance below the process average.

Z values can be used with a table of the standard normal distribution (Figure 6–14) to estimate the proportion of output that will be beyond any specification (an approximate value, assuming that the process is in statistical control and is normally distributed).

- For a unilateral tolerance, locate the value of Z along the edges of the table in Figure 6–14. The units and tenths digits are along the left edge, and the hundredths digit is along the top. The number found where this row and column intersect is p_z, the proportion out of specification. For instance, for $Z = 1.56$, the intersection of the 1.5 row and x.x6 column gives $p_z = .0594$, or about 6%.

- For a bilateral tolerance, calculate the proportions beyond upper and lower specification limits separately. For example, if Z_{USL} = 2.21 and Z_{LSL} = -2.85, the total beyond specification is $p_{zUSL} + p_{zLSL}$ = .0136 + .0022 = .0158, or about 1.6%.

The value Z_{min} can also be converted to a Capability Index, C_{pk}, defined as:

$$C_{pk} = \frac{Z_{min}}{3} = \text{Minimum of } \frac{USL - \overline{\overline{X}}}{3\hat{\sigma}} \text{ or } \frac{-(LSL - \overline{\overline{X}})}{3\hat{\sigma}}$$

where USL and LSL are the upper and lower engineering specifications, $\overline{\overline{X}}$ is the process average, and $\hat{\sigma}$ is the process standard deviation.

A process with Z_{min} = 3, which could be described as having $\overline{\overline{X}} \pm 3\sigma$ capability, would have a Capability Index C_{pk} = 1.00. If Z_{min} = 4, the process would have $\overline{\overline{X}} \pm 4\sigma$ capability and C_{pk} = 1.33.

4.c. Evaluate the Process Capability

At this point, the process has been brought into statistical control and its capability has been described in terms of Z_{min} or C_{pk}. The next step is to evaluate the process capability in terms of meeting customer requirements.

The fundamental goal is never-ending improvement in process performance. In the near-term, however, priorities must be set as to which processes should receive attention first. This is essentially an economic decision. The circumstances vary from case to case, depending on the nature of the particular process in question and the performance of other processes which might also be candidates for immediate improvement action.

While each such decision could be resolved individually, it is often helpful to use broader guidelines to set priorities and promote consistency of improvement efforts. Certain procedures may refer to across-the-board capability requirements of $\overline{\overline{X}} \pm 3\sigma$ capability and further specify $\overline{\overline{X}} \pm 4\sigma$ capability for new processes affecting Control Items or other significant product characteristics. These requirements are intended to assure a minimum performance level that is consistent among characteristics, products, and manufacturing sources.

Figure 6-14. Standard Normal Distribution and Normal Distribution.

P_z = the proportion of process output beyond a particular value of interest (such as a specification limit) that is z standard deviation units away from the process average (for a process that is in statistical control and is normally distributed). For example, if z = 2.17, P_z = .0150 or 1.5%. In any actual situation, this proportion is only approximate.

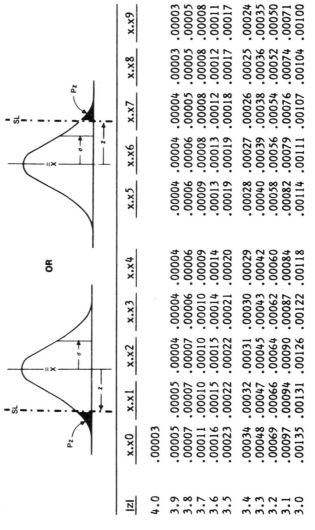

|z|	x.x0	x.x1	x.x2	x.x3	x.x4	x.x5	x.x6	x.x7	x.x8	x.x9
4.0	.00003									
3.9	.00005	.00005	.00004	.00004	.00004	.00004	.00004	.00004	.00003	.00003
3.8	.00007	.00007	.00007	.00006	.00006	.00006	.00006	.00005	.00005	.00005
3.7	.00011	.00010	.00010	.00010	.00009	.00009	.00008	.00008	.00008	.00008
3.6	.00016	.00015	.00015	.00014	.00014	.00013	.00013	.00012	.00012	.00011
3.5	.00023	.00022	.00022	.00021	.00020	.00019	.00019	.00018	.00017	.00017
3.4	.00034	.00032	.00031	.00030	.00029	.00028	.00027	.00026	.00025	.00024
3.3	.00048	.00047	.00045	.00043	.00042	.00040	.00039	.00038	.00036	.00035
3.2	.00069	.00066	.00064	.00062	.00060	.00058	.00056	.00054	.00052	.00050
3.1	.00097	.00094	.00090	.00087	.00084	.00082	.00079	.00076	.00074	.00071
3.0	.00135	.00131	.00126	.00122	.00118	.00114	.00111	.00107	.00104	.00100

z	.00	.01	.02	.03	.04	.05	.06	.07	.08	.09
2.9	.0019	.0018	.0018	.0017	.0016	.0016	.0015	.0015	.0014	.0014
2.8	.0026	.0025	.0024	.0023	.0023	.0022	.0021	.0021	.0020	.0019
2.7	.0035	.0034	.0033	.0032	.0031	.0030	.0029	.0028	.0027	.0026
2.6	.0047	.0045	.0044	.0043	.0041	.0040	.0039	.0038	.0037	.0036
2.5	.0062	.0060	.0059	.0057	.0055	.0054	.0052	.0051	.0049	.0048
2.4	.0082	.0080	.0078	.0075	.0073	.0071	.0069	.0068	.0066	.0064
2.3	.0107	.0104	.0102	.0099	.0096	.0094	.0091	.0089	.0087	.0084
2.2	.0139	.0136	.0132	.0129	.0125	.0122	.0119	.0116	.0113	.0110
2.1	.0179	.0174	.0170	.0166	.0162	.0158	.0154	.0150	.0146	.0143
2.0	.0228	.0222	.0217	.0212	.0207	.0202	.0197	.0192	.0188	.0183
1.9	.0287	.0281	.0274	.0268	.0262	.0256	.0250	.0244	.0239	.0233
1.8	.0359	.0351	.0344	.0336	.0329	.0322	.0314	.0307	.0301	.0294
1.7	.0446	.0436	.0427	.0418	.0409	.0401	.0392	.0384	.0375	.0367
1.6	.0548	.0537	.0526	.0516	.0505	.0495	.0485	.0475	.0465	.0455
1.5	.0668	.0655	.0643	.0630	.0618	.0606	.0594	.0582	.0571	.0559
1.4	.0808	.0793	.0778	.0764	.0749	.0735	.0721	.0708	.0694	.0681
1.3	.0968	.0951	.0934	.0918	.0901	.0885	.0869	.0853	.0838	.0823
1.2	.1151	.1131	.1112	.1093	.1075	.1056	.1038	.1020	.1003	.0985
1.1	.1357	.1335	.1314	.1292	.1271	.1251	.1230	.1210	.1190	.1170
1.0	.1587	.1562	.1539	.1515	.1492	.1469	.1446	.1423	.1401	.1379
0.9	.1841	.1814	.1788	.1762	.1736	.1711	.1685	.1660	.1635	.1611
0.8	.2119	.2090	.2061	.2033	.2005	.1977	.1949	.1922	.1894	.1867
0.7	.2420	.2389	.2358	.2327	.2297	.2266	.2236	.2206	.2177	.2148
0.6	.2743	.2709	.2676	.2643	.2611	.2578	.2546	.2514	.2483	.2451
0.5	.3085	.3050	.3015	.2981	.2946	.2912	.2877	.2843	.2810	.2776
0.4	.3446	.3409	.3372	.3336	.3300	.3264	.3228	.3192	.3156	.3121
0.3	.3821	.3783	.3745	.3707	.3669	.3632	.3594	.3557	.3520	.3483
0.2	.4207	.4168	.4129	.4090	.4052	.4013	.3974	.3936	.3897	.3859
0.1	.4602	.4562	.4522	.4483	.4443	.4404	.4364	.4325	.4286	.4247
0.0	.5000	.4960	.4920	.4880	.4840	.4801	.4761	.4721	.4681	.4641

Figure 6-15. Calculate the Process Capability.

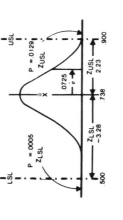

From the example:

$$\overline{\overline{X}} \; = \; .738$$

$$\hat{\sigma} \; = \; .0725$$

$$USL \; = \; .900$$

$$LSL \; = \; .500$$

- Since this process has bilateral tolerances:

$$Z_{USL} = \frac{USL - \overline{\overline{X}}}{\hat{\sigma}} = \frac{.900 - .738}{.0725} = \frac{.162}{.0725} = 2.23$$

$$Z_{LSL} = \frac{LSL - \overline{\overline{X}}}{\hat{\sigma}} = \frac{.500 - .738}{.0725} = \frac{-.238}{.0725} = -3.28$$

$$Z_{min} = 2.23$$

The proportions out of specification would be:

$$P_{Z_{USL}} \; = \; .0129 \text{ (from the table on the standard normal distribution in Figure 6-14)}$$

$$P_{Z_{LSL}} \; = \; .0005 \text{ (from the table on the standard normal distribution in Figure 6-14)}$$

$$P_{total} \; = \; .0134 \text{ (about 1.3%)}$$

The Capability Index would be:

$$C_{pk} = \frac{Z_{min}}{3} = \frac{2.23}{3} = .74$$

- If this process could be adjusted toward the center of the specification, the proportion of parts falling beyond either or both specification limits might be reduced, even with no change in $\hat{\sigma}$. For instance, if confirmed with control charts that $\overline{\overline{X}}_{new} = .700$ (centered), then:

$$Z_{USL} = \frac{USL - \overline{\overline{X}}_{new}}{\hat{\sigma}} = \frac{.900 - .700}{.0725} = \frac{.200}{.0725} = 2.76$$

$$Z_{LSL} = \frac{LSL - \overline{\overline{X}}_{new}}{\hat{\sigma}} = \frac{.500 - .700}{.0725} = \frac{-.200}{.0725} = -2.76$$

The total proportion out of specification would be:

$$Pz_{USL} + Pz_{LSL} = .0029 + .0029 = .0058 \text{ (about .6\%)}$$

The Capability Index would be:

$$C_{pk} = \frac{Z_{min}}{3} = \frac{2.76}{3} = .92$$

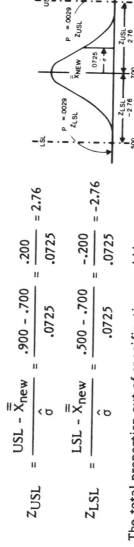

Whether in response to a capability criterion that has not been met, or to the continuing need for improvement of cost and quality performance even beyond minimum capability requirements, the action required is the same:

- Improve the process performance by reducing the variation that comes from common causes. This means taking management action to improve the system.

In those cases where more immediate action is necessary to meet short-term needs, two stop-gaps may be available:

- Sort output and scrap or rework as necessary (thus adding cost and tolerating waste).

- Alter the specifications for consistency with the process performance (thus not improving the performance the customer sees).

These are both clearly inferior to process improvement.

4.d. Improve the Process Capability

The problems causing unacceptable process capability are usually common causes. Actions must be directed toward the system—the underlying process factors which account for the process variability, such as machine performance, consistency of input materials, the basic methods by which the process operates, training methods, or the working environment. As a general rule, these system-related causes of process non-capability are beyond the abilities of operators or their local supervision to correct. Instead, they require management intervention to make basic changes, allocate resources, and provide the coordination needed to improve the process performance. Attempts to correct the system with short-range local actions will be unsuccessful.

4.e. Chart and Analyze the Revised Process

When systematic process actions have been taken, their effects should be apparent in the control chart, especially in terms of reduced ranges. The charts become a way of verifying the effectiveness of the action.

As the process change is implemented, the control chart should be monitored carefully. This change period can be disruptive to operations, potentially causing new control problems that could obscure the effect of the system change.

After any instabilities of the change period have been resolved, the new process capability should be assessed and used as the basis of new control limits for future operations.

7 CASES IN QUALITY CONTROL

SHELLER-GLOBE

Sheller-Globe, of Toledo, Ohio, supplies parts, components and assemblies for cars, trucks, and other vehicles to American and European automotive manufacturers. The company also manufactures and distributes such items as office products and accessories, microprocessor-based instruments and related equipment, nuclear-radiation monitoring systems, and special-purpose electronic components.

In early 1984, Sheller-Globe formally adopted their new Continuous Quality Improvement Program, known as CQI. In simple terms, CQI is a carefully planned process in which all employees in every part of the company are responsible for improving the quality of performance, service, and products at Sheller-Globe. People at Sheller-Globe consider the following to be the important elements of their CQI process:

—Employees at all levels are involved and participate in developing and executing quality control methods and ideas.
—Everyone continually practices careful control of what we do and how we do it.
—Product development is a cooperative effort with manufacturing. Quality assurance begins with each new idea.

—By being involved in continuous improvement, all employees will achieve personal growth and satisfaction. Continuous Quality Improvement applies to people, too.

—Formal training and education will be provided to all employees to prepare them to do their jobs better.

—Tools such as statistical quality control will be provided to and utilized by all employees.

—The next step in any process is our customer and that customer is number one.

—The constant guide for our work is plan, do, check, and take corrective action.

A two-day orientation to CQI for 130 managers from all segments of the company's operations initiated the program's implementation. Shortly afterward, twenty-seven key managers were sent to Japan to attend a series of lectures by noted Japanese authorities on organization and quality and to visit a number of leading Japanese manufacturing firms. In June of 1984, a group of the company's managers assembled in Toledo, Ohio, and signed Sheller-Globe's "Declaration of Commitment to Quality Performance."

Sheller-Globe established four steering groups to address particular aspects of the CQI process: (1) the Quality Control Circles Steering Group, which deals with employee involvement in the company's business; (2) the Statistical Process Controls Steering Group, which works to expand the application of statistical process control techniques throughout the company; (3) the Training and Education Steering Group, which determines the educational requirements of the corporation and develops effective training programs and courses; and (4) the Productivity and Compensation Steering Group, which studies various programs to improve productivity and efficiency throughout the company.

In addition to the steering groups, the Corporate CQI Council, comprised of six senior officers of the company, meets regularly to study and promote the CQI process and review the progress that is being made. These council members deal with employee orientation and participation, including the promotion and growth of quality control circles, dissemination of information on quality performance, and training in the application of statistical process control tools. They also prescribe actions to correct major chronic performance problems, such as ways to diminish cost-related customer complaints and reduce scrap and rework, and the use of project teams to address particular quality problems.

Sheller-Globe's Quality Control Circles

At Sheller-Globe, QC circles consist of groups of six to twelve people who do similar work and who normally work together. They generally meet one hour a week on company time to identify, analyze, and solve quality and work-related problems. Membership in these groups is strictly voluntary, and all Sheller-Globe employees eventually have the opportunity to join.

During the first ten meetings of an organized QC circle, members are taught basic problem-solving techniques. They learn how to identify, define, investigate, and analyze problems themselves, or they may request assistance from other departments for those areas beyond their abilities. Once they arrive at a workable solution to a problem, the circle members submit their findings and recommendations to management in a formal presentation.

Comprehensive training aids are used—at Sheller-Globe, the basic QC circles audiovisual course includes:

"Introduction to Quality Circles," providing information about organizing and maintaining a circle,

"Brainstorming," telling how to encourage creativity and generate the greatest number of solutions to a problem,

"Cause-and-Effect Diagrams," explaining these powerful aids to an organized approach to finding the true causes of problems,

"Pareto Diagrams," defining this means to identify the most important aspects of a problem,

"Histograms," providing a fundamental understanding of how to determine frequency distributions, which helps sort out likely causes of problems.

"Check sheets," discussing the need for accurate historical data and how to record it,

"Case Study," offering a real case history that utilizes all of the problem-solving techniques,

SHELLER-GLOBE CORPORATION

DECLARATION OF COMMITMENT TO QUALITY PERFORMANCE

We believe that QUALITY is the foundation for the long-term success of any business activity.

CONTINUOUS QUALITY IMPROVEMENT creates a chain reaction resulting in decreased costs by better utilizing human effort, equipment and materials as the defects in the system are eliminated. QUALITY IMPROVEMENT leads to greater productivity which, in turn, leads to larger market share with quality leadership and lower price.

Repetition of this reaction cycle assures continuance of the business, providing job security and the potential for more employment opportunities. It also leads to increased pride in workmanship, pride in the Company and pride in our accomplishments.

We believe that Sheller-Globe Corporation must adopt the management principles embodied in the attainment of the goal of CONTINUOUS QUALITY IMPROVEMENT, including the benefits of participation for each and every employee of the Company, and the commitment of financial resources to those principles.

We, the undersigned, hereby declare our commitment to CONTINUOUS QUALITY IMPROVEMENT in all areas and functions of the Company's activities, and to uncompromising effort to position Sheller-Globe as the recognized worldwide QUALITY LEADER in each of its continuing product classes, as measured and rated by its customers.

To produce a coordinated effort toward this commitment, we subscribe to and will incorporate the following PRINCIPLES OF MANAGEMENT LEADERSHIP in carrying out our ongoing responsibilities:

Figure 7-1. Declaration of Commitment to Quality Performance.

- Improvement of products and services requires constancy of purpose and continuous planning for the future.
- Constantly and forever improving the system of production and services to eliminate all forms of waste.
- Promotion of greater job satisfaction by reviewing with each employee what is specifically expected from the job and training each employee to be proficient at it.
- Improvement of supervision through training to help people and processes do a better job. Quality Control Circles are to be encouraged.
- Insisting that all causes of action be supported by analysis, facts and measurement – not by "experience" and intuition. Statistical analysis techniques will be used in all functions of the Company.
- Driving out fear through communications, teamwork and employee participation.
- The number of outside suppliers will be limited to those for which we have the resources to carry out continuous communication and the requirements of this Declaration.
- The guide for total management activity will be to PLAN, DO, CHECK the results and take corrective ACTION – P.D.C.A.

Individuals exhibit extraordinary performance when a sense of personal accomplishment and importance exists. The extent to which an individual can improve his or her contribution may be very small, yet the sum of these added together will make the difference between a quality organization and a mediocre one.

"We are dedicated to building a quality organization through developing quality people who produce quality products for our customers."

"Graphs," teaching the various forms of graphs and their advantages over tabular data,

"Management Presentations," training a QC circle to organize and present its cases to management for recognition, approval, and implementation, and

"Advanced Training," introducing statistical techniques to a circle after members have mastered the basic problem-solving techniques.

The organization of a QC circles program in a Sheller-Globe facility first involves the appointment of a facilitator and the formation of a steering advisory committee made up of representatives from various areas of the facility. The facilitator coordinates all circle activities, as well as communications among the circles, the steering advisory committee, and management. He or she also trains circle leaders and publicizes circle activities inside and outside the company. The steering advisory committee is responsible for establishing program policies, procedures, objectives, and resources. The committee also directs the programs, meeting regularly with the facilitator to carry out plans.

Introduction of the process involves a one-day executive orientation seminar for plant staff and union executives (in unionized plants), a two-day orientation for middle management and union representatives, a two-day training session to present the philosophy and techniques of QC circles to company and union management, a three-day extensive training seminar for circle leaders, a one-day circle launch orientation, a three-day group dynamics session for circle leaders and company and union management, and a final review to the steering advisory committee.

Extensive instruction in the tools and applications of statistical process control, or SPC, has been provided since the company implemented a formal SPC program in early 1982. Check sheets, cause-and-effect diagrams, graphs, Pareto diagrams, histograms, scatter diagrams, and control charts are widely used throughout the company. With these tools, employees learn how to control variations within the manufacturing process by distinguishing between the few important problems and the trivial many that can affect the stability of the process. Results are then measured against realistic, meaningful levels of past performance with the objective of achieving stable, predictable process control.

SPC has proven effective in helping to solve processing, manufacturing, and quality problems, as well as reducing scrap and rework. In some areas of Sheller-Globe, statistics have helped establish the need for better controls on equipment; in others, people at all levels have become much more conscious of process variabilities that cause problems leading to high scrap and rework. And SPC profits the workers as well. As Chester Gadzinski, chairman of the Statistical Process Control Steering Group, states: "An important benefit of an SPC program is that the control of a process is given back to the equipment operator, making routine jobs interesting and challenging." Among the success stories, three serve to illustrate what SPC has done for Sheller-Globe.

At the company's Iowa City plant, shrinkage of the vinyl cover stock used to vacuum-form the outer skins of an automotive padded part was a major problem. Through statistical techniques, employees discovered that a shorter heating cycle at a higher temperature was the solution. As a result, shrinkage was minimized, and the scrap rate reduced by 86 percent.

At the company's Montpelier, Indiana, plant, which makes extruded rubber seals and weatherstripping, one rubber compound began curing before it was extruded. Control charts used to monitor temperature variations in the Banbury mixing equipment that compounds batches of rubber material for extruding showed that the process was out of control. By reducing the size of the batch in the Banbury mixer, less mixing time was required and the stability of the material increased. The end result was a 2 percent increase in productivity.

The company's Hardy plant in Union City, Indiana, has reduced scrap and rework in a number of areas through the use of statistics. In one operation involving the manufacture of rearview-mirror assemblies, SPC techniques helped bring about a 50 percent reduction in scrap.

Top management plays a vital role in directing Sheller-Globe's quality efforts. The company's QC circles are fully supported by its corporate staff, plant managers, supervisors, and union leaders. Armed with the allowed ample time to complete their projects, proper problem-solving tools, and surrounded by a supportive environment, Sheller-Globe's QC circle members are capable of solving nearly every problem they address.

Jack Henkaline, manager of employee involvement for Sheller-Globe, avows:

> Throughout Sheller-Globe, organized employee involvement programs affirm the belief that those people who do a job can best suggest changes for improving the job. Employee involvement programs also provide a channel for employees to make improvements on projects that they are interested in, creating a winning situation for everyone. . . . Employee involvement is a bold step forward in recognizing the dignity of people and the jobs they perform.[1]

Education and Training

Competing through quality requires an educated work force equipped to deal with the challenges of new technology, tough competition, and a demanding customer base. Sheller-Globe has launched a new educational program designed to provide all of its employees with broad skills and knowledge in particular to their jobs, as well as in certain areas of statistical process control, basic manufacturing processes, communication, and teamwork. Heavy emphasis is placed on job-skills training, retraining, and reorientation, and on continuing education for technical and professional personnel. Such comprehensive training programs are viewed as the key to the continuous improvements in the company's productivity and manufacturing processes that will enable Sheller-Globe to be more competitive.

Nestled within the company's corporate INSIGHT publication is the following proclamation:

> As a company, a plant, or as individuals, we cannot be satisfied with just getting by. We must constantly strive to do things better.
>
> We must be willing to share our vast energies, ideas, and abilities.
>
> By making constant individual improvement, everyone benefits from a committed, versatile, trained group of people working together to improve our methods of meeting customer needs. By learning and acquiring new ideas and skills, we will be better able to pursue new opportunities. We must strive to upgrade our skills. We can and should expect this from each other.
>
> We must be able to rely on our fellow employees to do their jobs right the first time in order to meet our customers' needs.[2]

Employees appear to be reacting positively to the CQI program. A large number are impressed by top management's participation in the program and commitment to employee involvement. As Shirley Roubnik, a lead inspector at Sheller-Globe Engineered Polymers Company in Arizona, puts it: "The program is very near and dear to me because of what I do. It involves everyone, including management, and I like that." Ray Holloman, a diecut machine operator from Bristol, Pennsylvania, describes CQI as "a splendid program." He claims: "Many times in the past we've had different problems we've wanted to talk about, but nobody wanted to hear. Before you can arrive at a solution, you have to acknowledge the problem. Overall with this program, things will be much better."

Before CQI was implemented, problems were unclearly defined, and workers on the production line were rarely consulted about solutions. With CQI, all that has changed. Roger Zimmerman, quality control manager at Victoreen, Inc., Sheller-Globe's subsidiary in Cleveland, Ohio, explains, "We've never used this kind of common-sense approach. If you use the basic tools of statistical process control, you can solve 95 percent of the problems. It's much easier to concentrate on and identify problems. Everybody's starting to feel that."

So far, it appears that CQI really does pinpoint problems as they occur, really does give workers the feeling that their bosses are listening to them and are willing to act upon their suggestions, and really does make a difference in the quality of the product. Although the program is still in its early stages. Gary Snook, industrial engineering supervisor at the Norwalk, Ohio, Assembly Plant is amazed how well everyone seems to accept it. He exclaims: "There's excitement and a cooperative attitude, and I'm glad to be a part of it."

GENERAL MOTORS

General Motors has embarked on a "Journey to World Class Quality." In March of 1981 it established the office of Vice President of Quality and Reliability to highlight the importance of corporate quality. Top management has deepened its commitment by creating a corporate Quality and Reliability Group, a GM Quality Council, which meets bimonthly and bears final responsibility for quality, and a Steering Committee, consisting of all the group vice presidents who meet monthly to recommend quality policy to the council. General

Motors also holds annual executive Quality Conferences to convey its quality message and goals to its top managers worldwide.

The Crosby methods of quality management, developed by Philip Crosby and taught at the Crosby College in Winter Park, Florida, are an integral part of GM's program. Crosby encourages management to become committed to the quality process by issuing a corporate quality policy, ensuring that the message of quality is communicated throughout the company, and making quality number one on the agenda of regular management status meetings. He also suggests that quality improvement teams and quality councils be established, and he stresses the benefits of employee education and employee recognition.

Crosby defines quality in terms of four absolutes. Absolute number one states: "The definition of quality is conformance to requirements."[3] Crosby insists that employees must know the standards they are expected to achieve. Not only should management set and clearly communicate requirements concerning materials finishes, acceptable tolerance levels, and so forth, but it must also provide the necessary resources, training, and assistance to allow employees to do things right—the first time.

Doing things right the first time requires prevention, not detection, which leads to Crosby's second absolute: "The system of quality is prevention."[4] Inspection never did solve the problem of producing defects and never will. Increased employee involvement in the manufacturing process, however, can help. For example, training in the techniques of statistical process control enables workers to identify the variables that cause the process to move out of control and allows them to take corrective actions.

Crosby's third absolute of quality is "The performance standard is zero defects."[5] Saying "that's close enough" or being satisfied with a merely "acceptable" quality level indicates that management has second-rate expectations expressed as vague guidelines. People will perform to the standard they are given as long as they understand it, but standards like "excellence," "acceptable quality levels," and "pride," in Crosby's opinion, are nonspecific and result in uneven quality.

Crosby divides the cost of quality into two components: the price of nonconformance and the price of conformance. The price of nonconformance includes the expenses that arise from doing things wrong—rework, scrap, warranty claims, engineering change orders, and so forth—which can total 20 percent or more of sales in manufacturing companies. The price of conformance consists of the costs of doing things right—training in quality education, preventive maintenance, supplier quality seminars, and so on—which, in a well-run company, average about 3 to 4 percent of sales. To allay the high costs of nonconformance, Crosby issues his fourth absolute: "The measurement of quality is the price of nonconformance."[6] Thus, the price of nonconformance can be used as an indicator of quality improvement and of opportunities for corrective action.

Following the Crosby methods, General Motors has established several objectives on its Journey to World Class Quality. D. H. McPherson, vice president of Quality and Reliability and Service Parts Operations for GM, describes these objectives as follows: [7]

1. We require that quality be an integral part of the planning process. General Motors is broken down into a number of business units—each of which submits a five-year strategic business plan. Quality plans are a major part of all business plans.

2. Make education for quality a mechanism for quality improvement. For example, 2800 GM executives have completed the Philip Crosby Quality College Courses in Florida. That number is increased through our own Quality Institute jointly established with the Philip Crosby Association in Michigan, which offers a 4½ day Crosby Quality Management Course.

3. We have zeroed in on Four Key Success Factors for quality. The first is management commitment. It has always been Phil Crosby's contention that if you don't have this you won't have quality. You can no longer "turn a quality problem over to the quality people." It's management's job to get involved with quality—organize it—set requirements—provide resources—establish leadership—and do the missionary work and followup. Top management's personal participation sends the message that quality is the first consideration. At General Motors, executives are urged to ask the right questions to convey their participation:

- Are they asking their staffs about the understanding of the four absolutes of quality?
- Are they asking for their specific quality improvement plans—for service AND manufacturing—the whole process?
- Are they asking about a list of top quality issues and the progress being made to solve them?
- Are they asking for objective progress assessments of ALL functions, including their own staff's?
- Are they asking for the price of non-conformance?

- Are they asking for routine periodic quality improvement reviews?
- Are they asking for action plans for suppliers relative to quality improvement?

The second key success factor is people involvement in a positive environment, with no blame setting and no taboos. No one can be left out of the quality loop. That means EVERYONE, not just the production workers.

This is a major cultural change. One of the biggest problems we have is convincing people that quality is not just product related. Mistakes are mistakes and waste is waste whether made by mechanics, salespeople, or even financial people.

The third key success factor is quality performance processes. Each task and activity must have processes and the tools to ensure conformance to specifications and requirements. This means that management must provide for continuous quality improvement in the office as well as in the plant. To accomplish this we must think in terms of prevention at the very first opportunity, not after critical activities and events have already taken place.

The fourth key success factor is customer satisfaction. Here our resolve is to make GM the world leader in quality, reliability, durability, performance, service, and value, as confirmed by customer defined measures and marketplace response.

4. The fourth objective of GM's Journey to World Class Quality deals with specific ambitious goals for conformance to specification. That's another Crosby principle which does away with those awful three letter words: "that's close enough." Our aim is to have engineering and manufacturing agree to the product specification, and never deviate.

5. Elimination of incoming inspection of material, particularly of material made by GM for GM. If the receiving area can find defects then it's certainly obvious that the sender can eliminate defects. Inspecting out defects is not the ultimate objective. The ultimate objective is to do it right the first time. Prevention systems address errors BEFORE they occur to enable management teams to achieve that ultimate objective.

Quality improvement processes at GM reveal that the company is off to a good start in managing change. At one GM plants that manufactures nearly 1,400 different plastic parts, a quality improvement process combining Crosby methods, people involvement, participative management, and statistical process control has yielded an improved overall Corporate Quality Audit, a marked decline in customer returns, greater plant-wide efficiency, and major cost savings. And, thanks to quality improvement processes, the Pontiac Grand Am, Oldsmobile Calais, and Buick Somerset Regal received the highest customer acceptance rating at introduction of any new GM passenger car.

General Motors has designed its new Saturn project as a model for attaining world class quality. GM envisions the Saturn Corporation as having a twofold mission:

1. To create a world class quality vehicle competitive with the most efficient small car producers by using the latest in electronic business systems and enlightened manager-employee relationships and

2. To become a learning laboratory to make all of GM's operations world class.

Crosby's quality improvement methods will form the basis for company-wide quality control efforts. First, all of Saturn's management who have not yet attended the Crosby College will be enrolled to study Crosby methods. Thereafter, GM plans to educate 100 percent of Saturn's employees in quality control through the GM Quality Institute.

GM's Journey to World Class Quality involves teamwork, attention to detail, and continual reevaluation of its efforts. The journey cannot be made overnight, but GM is convinced that its determination to succeed will make the expedition most productive.

FLORIDA POWER AND LIGHT COMPANY

The Florida Power and Light Company (FPL), Florida's largest electric utility, supplies two-thirds of the state with electricity. In terms of customers serviced, it is the country's fifth largest investor-owned electric utility. Since 1981, when its Quality Improvement Program (QIP) was established, FPL has been providing its customers with services and products of increasingly higher quality. Indeed, when internationally recognized quality consultant Dr. Joseph M. Juran visited FPL, he credited them with having the most outstanding quality improvement program of any service industry in the United States.

Since its founding in 1925, FPL has grown to become a leader in the industry, consistently providing its customers with quality service and reliability. In the 1970s, however, FPL found it increasingly difficult to keep costs down. Rapid population growth forced the company to expend much of its capital in new construction. With escalating fuel prices and high interest rates compounding the problem, management had no choice but to raise utility rates to help cover the expenses. Naturally, customers objected, and it soon became obvious to the company that something had to be done.

At this time, management realized that internal improvements in quality and productivity would ultimately benefit customers, employees, and shareholders alike. Armed with the theories of such experts as Deming, Crosby, and Juran, FPL decided to make quality its primary objective. "Then came the very difficult process of adapting quality improvement principles designed primarily for manufacturing to a service industry," said FPL's president, John J. Hudiburg.[8]

Undaunted by the challenge, FPL decided to develop its own program, utilizing the best available approaches and concepts. To assure total commitment, management of the implementing departments set up task teams consisting of first-line supervisors to determine what type of quality program would be most effective for them. Team participants ranked two to three levels below department head, but their policy recommendations would affect every decision.

The company's quality improvement program was formally initiated in the office of Marshall McDonald, FPL's chairman of the board. In early 1981, he described FPL's new quality philosophy:

> I think it is time for American industry across the board, from widget manufacturers to those of us in the power and energy industry, to learn how to provide products and services that are right the first time around. We do not need to spend billions on fixing products after they are produced imperfectly. We have been looking at the horse from the wrong end. We have been concerned with keeping rejects down rather than eliminating them completely. We have been busy keeping imperfection under control rather than producing perfection.
>
> American companies (including Florida Power and Light Company) can improve dramatically when we make up our minds to improve, and when we have the proper motivation and leadership. Utility companies can supply power and provide reliable service—the first time. It's all a matter of attitude.[9]

McDonald then announced a "permanent attitude change at Florida Power & Light Company," stating that "this Quality Program will affect the efforts of everyone in our Company, from the chairman's office throughout the total system." Both union and nonunion workers responded, having had positive experiences from previous pilot programs. He challenged all of FPL's 13,691 employees (salary and hourly, union and nonunion) to "reach inside yourselves from this day on and summon the very best and the highest that is in us. As of this moment, quality is our highest banner and standard."[10]

At FPL, quality is defined as "conformance to valid requirements," reflecting management's belief that the classical notion of quality as the degree of conformance to a standard is too narrow. W. Kent Sterett, FPL's QIP manager, explains:

> "Valid" deals with the realism and currency of the requirement and the concept that quality is the degree of user satisfaction. In other words, the customer determines whether or not quality has been achieved. We also realize that the "customer" is the person or department which uses an employee's service or product, not just the rate payer. Thus, the same measure— customer satisfaction—applies throughout the company.[11]

The Eight Steps to Quality

Management laid out the new "Eight Steps to Quality," which constitute a system designed to increase communication throughout the company, improve quality, and, ultimately, reduce operating costs and customer electric rates.

1. Management Commitment.   Studies have shown that 80 percent of problems resulting from poor quality must be handled by management; only 20 percent can be solved by the workers alone. From the start, FPL's management has been committed to developing and guiding its quality improvement program, for "without management support at all levels, it is unlikely the program will be taken seriously throughout the corporate structure."[12] Top executives acknowledged early on that "when the program is being introduced into an organization, representatives from all levels of management must be involved so they can claim ownership. In this way they will not perceive this to be just another 'Ivory Tower' program from the General Office."[13]

2. Quality Improvement Teams.   Teamwork characterizes FPL's approach to quality improvement. According to top-level management, their program "acknowledges that no one is an island, that everyone must work together to meet our corporate quality objectives." In December 1982, twenty months after the start of the program, 400 QIP teams had been established throughout the company. By August of 1984, when the number of teams at FPL had grown to 640, Sterett announced that the company's year-end goal was to have 800 teams operating "at every location from the Georgia border to the Florida Keys, from the chairman of the board to the lineman up the pole."[15] By the end of 1985, more than 1,300 teams had been formed at FPL, made up of voluntary members from all organizational levels. At the very top, a Quality Council was established, consisting of fifteen senior managers, among them department vice presidents, functional area directors, and the director of nuclear affairs. This council meets to develop and then evaluate overall policies and goals. All department and staff activities are thus tied together at the director and vice-president level.

Supporting the corporate activity is a QIP Staff Development Team, comprised of people from the training and quality engineering departments, the QIP staff group, and others with expertise in management and information systems. This team plans and maintains the overall Corporate Quality Improvement Program and provides for training, support, and coordination between departments and the QIP staff group.

Six Corporate Issue Teams were also set up to give upper and middle management an opportunity to respond to issues that affect the entire company. Topics for discussion are selected through nominations from all the managers and then addressed by those managers who have volunteered to serve on solution-searching teams. In addition, corporate issue teams may recommend major changes in corporate policies and systems.

At the lowest level of the company, local quality improvement teams headed by a work group leader identify and solve problems lying within the employees' control. They select the problems they wish to work on and use team problem-solving techniques to come up with solutions and ideas for improvement. Whenever problems cross functional boundaries and cannot be solved at the local level, they're forwarded to cross-functional teams comprised of members from different work groups or departments. Led by managers and made up of the heads of the lower-level teams, these cross-functional team members can approach problem-solving with broader perspectives. Efforts are made to identify interfunctional improvements that will affect the members' immediate operations. Members are then responsible for coordinating the interaction of their respective local team members with those in other departments.

A quality improvement Lead Team oversees these functional and cross-functional teams. Headed by a director or vice president and composed of department managers representing each function within the organizational group, this team establishes organizational policy and procedures and evaluates the effectiveness of their overall program. In addition, whenever the local and cross-functional teams are unable to handle a problem, the appropriate manager on the Lead Team assumes responsibility for the resolution.

3. Management Orientation and Training.   In-house training sessions on the company's QIP philosophy, processes, and implementation are provided for facilitators and team leaders. Topics for study include methods for determining and analyzing root causes of problems, group dynamics, and techniques on analyzing information for team decisionmaking. In addition, lead team members study FPL's QIP philosophy in order to reach a consensus on its meaning and validity.

4. Economic Analyses.   In order to identify and select the most profitable opportunities for improvement, QIP participants are encouraged to perform regular economic analyses of the costs of quality. Initially, they learn to determine the costs of internal and external failure. When internal failures occur, costs are measured in terms of corrective action, redesign, turnover rates, purchase order rewrites, invalid or obsolete procedures, and tracking of system failures. External failure costs stem from billing errors, excessive maintenance, time and travel spent on rework, service liabilities, premature equipment failures, and changes made by customers due to the failure to meet user requirements.

As QIP team participants start to excel in conducting economic analyses on failure costs, they learn how to measure the costs of "preventative measures" and "quality appraisal." The costs of preventative measures include the time and effort spent on such efforts as specification reviews, training, manuals and procedures, vendor review and approval, interviewing job applicants, cost benefit analyses and improvements. Quality appraisals involve the costs required for supervisors to oversee the work of their subordinates, audits or evaluations, personnel appraisals, tests or pilot programs, inspection programs, vendor surveys, and charting trends.

5. *Identification of Root Causes.* Any procedures, specifications, plans, or processes that deviate from "valid" requirements prevent FPL from delivering high quality electrical service. Team members establish measurement standards based on valid requirements, which are used to track deviations. The standards establish guidelines for evaluating corrective actions. Should a product that either fails or becomes excessively costly still conform to requirements, team members are encouraged to question their validity.

6. *Corrective Action.* Each QIP team member seeks solutions that effectively and permanently solve root-cause problems. Solutions are tested on trial bases under actual working conditions. Should a solution prove successful, it may be implemented whenever required, after appropriate approval. Upper-level supervisors, managers, or even entire teams may be summoned for assistance if any lower-level teams lack the authority to take corrective action.

7. *Team Awareness of How Their Efforts Fit into Departmental and Corporate Goals.* FPL advertises its teams' successes through a monthly video program and company newspaper in order to promote employee involvement and awareness of the QIP program. According to Sterett, "the goal is total quality involvement," which means that every process, every job, and every person is consistently moving toward continuous improvement. "Quality," he claims, "is too important to take second place to anything else." [16]

Furthermore, all managers have been asked to set priorities for their "critical to quality" operations, formulate their goals for improvement, and measure the progress they've made toward reaching those goals.

8. *Recognizing High-Quality Performance as a Means of Motivation.* At FPL, outstanding team members are recognized in a variety of ways, ranging from a pat on the back, to a luncheon invitation with

a manager or supervisor, to formal banquets with Chairman McDonald and other top-level officials. Families of the team members are invited to the dinners, and awards of congratulations come packaged, quite appropriately, in table lamps designed from antique electric meters.

Quality, it seems to President John J. Hudiburg, is contagious. Throughout the state of Florida, several cities have adapted FPL's quality improvement program to their own uses to improve public services without passing the costs on to the taxpayers. According to Hudiburg, "We don't need any more proof that quality and productivity improvement is the wave of the future." [17]

THE QUALITY CIRCLES APPROACH TO EMPLOYEE INVOLVEMENT AT GTE

The development of employee involvement team approaches in the U.S. since the 1970s has spanned a wide range of orientations. Some approaches are patterned after the Japanese statistical quality control circles (QCC), with their sharp focus on quality. Others, frequently called quality of work life (QWL) groups, are usually associated with labor relations and concern themselves primarily with problems involving the work environment and work relationships. The focus of the activity of these EI approaches thus ranges from an association with highly structured problem solving (using statistical process control techniques to solve product quality related problems) to broad discussions of general environmental conditions in the workplace. Quality Circles at GTE have, from their beginnings in 1981, endeavored to strike a balance between these extremes by emphasizing both team building/team leadership skills and the systematic identification, analysis and solution of work-related problems.

GTE Quality Circles are voluntary, work group teams of non-supervisory GTE employees involved in the systematic identification, analysis, and solution of work related problems involving the goods or services they provide as well as their work environments. GTE Circle members follow an orderly problem solving model and utilize specific team problem solving techniques. Most GTE Quality Circle efforts thus draw effectively upon both the effects of good teamwork, and the benefits of following a systematic problem solving approach to achieve results which include: reaching consensus, building support for decisions, solving problems and providing members the "intrinsic rewards" which result from participation in the solution of meaningful problems. Employee involvement in the GTE Circles problem solving process meets both important organizational needs, and critical developmental and job enrichment needs of our employees, resulting in a "people building" orientation to improving organizational effectiveness.

The information in this section is excerpted from a November 1984 GTE Service Corporation company booklet, entitled *The Quality Circles Approach to Employee Involvement at GTE*, by Daniel M. Falvey, Manager, Organization Effectiveness, GTE Service Corporation, Stamford, Connecticut.

Key Characteristics and Fundamentals for Success

Listed below are seven key characteristics which we have found to be critical to a successful GTE Circles implementation and an effective ongoing Quality Circle process:

1. *Supervisor is Sponsor and Initial Circle Leader.* To enhance the cooperative relationship between employees and their supervisors, to help the Circle members get their problem solutions implemented and to develop the participative style of the supervisor.

2. *Voluntary.* For middle managers and supervisors to sponsor a Circle, for members to join and for the Circles to have free choice to work on any given work related problem.

3. *Solve Work Related Problems.* So the members can get satisfaction from productive problem solving and the organization can benefit from the members' ideas.

4. *Consensus Based Team Decision Process.* Which, while not appropriate in all decision-making situations, in the Quality Circle setting, enhances the team process and the quality of team decisions and problem solutions, as well as building the support of all members to the team's decisions.

5. *Senior Management Steering Committee Representing All Major Functions.* So location management uniformly understands, sponsors, guides and supports the Quality Circle activities on a sustained basis.

6. *Designated Full-Time Quality Circle Coordinator/Facilitator.* As an indication of management's willingness to truly support Quality Circles and a way to provide Circles, leaders, and managers with the amount and variety of support they need.

7. *No Direct Financial Rewards.* So members are motivated to join for self-improvement and for the intrinsic rewards of recognition and satisfaction which result from solving work related problems of interest to them. Where employee involvement approaches which include financial rewards (such as suggestion programs) already exist, it is important to differentiate between these approaches and GTE Circles in documents such as the Quality Circle Charter or Company Policies and Procedures related to Employee Involvement.

Potential Pitfalls

Based on our experience, we feel that with few exceptions, Quality Circle implementations which depart from the above listed "Key Characteristics" can lead to an ineffective or short lived Quality Circle process.

In addition, our experience has shown that a number of things can occur in even the most supportive, organizationally ready environments which can threaten the success of the Quality Circle process. These potential pitfalls include:

Top Management Change. Change in management can lead to concerns as to whether or not employee involvement and Quality Circles will remain a high priority. Effective transition management coupled with consultation which leads to early, informed and visible support by the new manager can generally avoid this pitfall.

Loss of Original Coordinator/Facilitator. Whether due to promotion, resignation, transfer or other reasons, loss of the original (and to a lesser extent, the succeeding) Quality Circles Coordinator/Facilitator is a difficult trauma for the Circles process. Quick action in identifying and training a suitable interim and/or replacement Coordinator is essential. Outstanding Circle leaders are logical candidates for the Coordinator role in many instances.

Change in the Work Group Supervisor/Initial Quality Circle Leader and Sponsor. Through a combination of proper selection and training, the problems caused by the need to replace a Circle leader can be tempered. There is evidence that the Circle process can be self-healing in some instances where participation in Quality Circle activity has helped surface an employee/member with high potential for Circle leadership.

Need to Cut Period Costs; Elimination of the Coordinator/Facilitator Position. Due to its staff orientation, when budget crunches occur, the role of Quality Circle Coordinator is sometimes jeopardized. Prioritization of the employee involvement process and creativity in maintaining a designated Coordinator are required of a location's management to avoid this potential fatal pitfall.

Resistance to Change. Resistance to change in the form of employee objections to Circles can occur early and openly. An example would be when employees express concerns about job security which could result from productivity gains made by Circles. Or, resistance can occur a year or more later, and be far more subtle. For example, mid-managers may begin to withdraw support and shift priorities away from employee involvement when the novelty of Circles has worn off, and traditional areas of mid-management concern become of interest to the maturing Circles.

Logistics. Shift rotation, very small work groups, employee transfers and "bumping," work force reductions, "ship week," and multi-shift and continuous operations are only a few of the logistical problems which make it difficult for Quality Circles to form, train, meet regularly and maintain their membership. Throughout GTE, myriad creative solutions to difficult problems like these have been found, and in only a very few instances where there has been dedicated effort has it proven impossible to implement and maintain effective Circles.

Fundamentals for Success

Three fundamentals underlie the success of GTE Circles: readiness, training and reinforcement. The primary fundamental underlying the success of GTE Circles is the accurate assessment of the factors affecting an organization's overall *readiness* (ability and willingness to initiate and sustain the implementation of GTE Circles) and, within the organization, the identification of the specific work groups which are best suited to early Quality Circle participation.

To treat the first of these issues, overall organizational readiness, a pair of informational/diagnostic approaches have been developed to assist a GTE unit in making an appropriate decision regarding the adoption of the Quality Circles approach to employee involvement:

The Management Overview. A two to three hour presentation of the GTE Quality Circle process by GTE's corporate Quality Circle Training and Communications staff designed to give a location's top management a balanced exposure to both the potential benefits and the realistic commitments which are generally required for a successful, sustained implementation of Quality Circles.

Key Readiness Factors Assessment. A sixteen-point readiness assessment instrument is used in a variety of structured data gathering and organizational self assessment manners to evaluate the organization's overall preparation for the implementation of GTE Circles. These readiness factors include:

1. Top management's understanding and support
2. Top management's own management style
3. Top management's goals for Circles
4. Middle management's attitude toward participative management
5. Interpersonal interaction
6. Two-way communication
7. Interpersonal skills of supervisors and managers
8. Commitment of required resources
9. Commitment to a realistic time frame
10. Distribution of power and trust; freedom to innovate
11. Organizational support
12. Availability of effective coordinator candidate
13. Union acceptance/contract limitations
14. Labor-management relations
15. History of "programs"
16. Organizational predictability and continuity

The second key readiness issue, the identification of specific work groups ready to be formed into the initial Circles, is assessed as follows:

Work Group Readiness Assessment. The work group readiness assessment is usually performed by the management, Quality Circle steering committee and Quality Circle coordinator at a location (with the consultation of GTE's corporate Quality Circle Training and Communications staff, as required). This assessment is aimed at identification of the specific work groups or areas within a given GTE location which are most appropriate for the initial placement and/or for likely expansion of GTE Circles. A model has been developed to assist with this critical readiness assessment activity (Figure 7-2).

The second fundamental underlying the success of GTE Quality Circles is *training*—at all levels and with a variety of purposes in building an effective, well supported Quality Circle process.

There is a popular scenario which envisions a group of interested and/or concerned employees assembled and charged with the responsibility of solving an important work related problem and invariably succeeding. We view that scenario as basically wishful thinking fueled

Figure 7-2.   Work Group Readiness for Quality Circles.

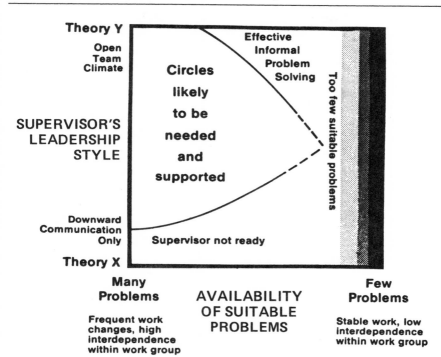

Source: Daniel M. Falvey, *The Quality Circles Approach to Employee Management at GTE* (Stamford, Conn.: GTE Service Corporation, 1984).

by at best sporadic (although occasionally dramatic) successes of "short cut" employee involvement efforts.

Studies of Quality Circle successes and failures in companies throughout the U.S. consistently report that the single factor most critical to the success of employee involvement problem solving efforts is training—especially the extent and quality of the leader and member training available and utilized in establishing the problem solving teams.

At GTE, the extensive training involved in the implementation of GTE Quality Circles evolves in tiers through the three to six month implementation process.

Tier 1: Top Management Overview—A two to three (or more) hour conference with a location's top management to explore the Quality Circle concept's requirements and potential benefits.

Tier 2: Steering Committee Workshop—A one day session which combines discussion of both conceptual and tactical implementation issues. These issues include training in Circle problem solving processes and techniques, goal clarification, role clarification (steering committee vis à vis management, coordinator, leaders, etc.) and initial implementation planning (initial Circle work groups, coordinator selection, policies and procedures, publicity, etc.)

Tier 3: Coordinator/Facilitator Training—Cross training with Corporate Quality Circle Training and and Communications during the Management Orientations, Management Workshops and Leader Training; a highly specific one day GTE Quality Circle Facilitation Skills Workshop and/or a five day more general Quality Circle Coordinator Training course.

Tier 4: Middle Management Overviews—One to two hour briefings to extend ownership of the Quality Circles to management at levels between those who attended the Top Management Orientation and those in first line supervision.

Tier 5: Middle Management Workshops—A one-half day concentrated session designed to build high support of the Quality Circle process among the managers of the supervisors who are potential initial Circle leaders.

Tier 6: Supervisor/Leader Training—Three days of Quality Circle techniques and leadership skills training for roughly twice the number of first line supervisors as can initially be supported as Circle leaders; serves to broaden ownership as well as produce a ready pool of trained leaders for replacement or expansion Circles and substitutes for the initial Circle leaders when absences are unavoidable.

Tier 7: Employee/Member Training—Done by supervisors/leaders of work groups in which enough (generally 5-10) employees have volunteered to become Circle members; typically takes first five to seven one hour Circle meetings.

The third, and, in terms of both initiating and sustaining the GTE Circle process, perhaps most important underlying fundamental is *reinforcement.* The importance of reinforcement is twofold:

1. Employees/Circle members need early and consistent assurance that the Circle process is a relevant one, participation in which is both encouraged and valued by management at all levels of the organization. The primary rewards for Quality Circle participation are the satisfaction which results from solving work related problems of importance to the Circle members, and the recognition from management associated with such accomplishments, and;

2. To be truly supportive, management needs evidence that the Circle process is genuinely contributing to the achievement of the mission, goals, and objectives of the business unit.

Without this two-way reinforcement, employees will either not join or will gradually lose interest in Circle participation because they perceive that the activity is window-dressing, or worse, that Circles are a manipulative device driven by strictly productivity improvement (even potential job elimination) management motivations. From management's standpoint, unless there are visible results of the Circles' impact on business related factors (quality, cost, etc.) within a reasonable length of time, interest in supporting or even allowing the Circle activity will eventually wane.

On an ongoing basis, the major vehicle for ensuring consistent two way reinforcement is the Management Presentation. This is normally a thirty minute or less meeting between appropriate management representatives and a team of Quality Circle members in which each member makes a brief contribution to the presentation. The members describe in a concise and businesslike manner the problem they selected, the process the members followed in solving it, the solution they implemented or are recommending and the results they have achieved or expect to achieve.

Periodic Management Presentations serve to continually demonstrate to management that the Circles' efforts are productive and that in most cases, the Circles are developing into skillful problem solving and prevention teams. These presentations also serve as an opportunity for Circle members to reap the rewards of accomplishment, self-satisfaction and recognition from meeting with management to present their ideas and accomplishments.

Roles and Processes

Ideally, *everyone* at a GTE Quality Circle location should feel involved in the process. Responsibility for the implementation of GTE Circles should be distributed so as to avoid the creation of cliques and to prevent the Circles from otherwise acting as a divisive force among employees or functional work groups.

Figure 7-3 below illustrates the distinct roles key individuals and groups play in implementing GTE Circles. Once established, Quality Circles become a part of the way a location operates, gradually forming the culture of the organization. Over time, the roles may thus become more flexible, and the distinctions between them may soften, as when a member emerges to act as Circle leader for a time or when a Circle reaches a level of maturity at which it can operate effectively with only intermittent or no facilitative assistance.

GTE Circles are typically comprised of five to ten volunteer, non-supervisory employees from the same work group who meet each week for one hour on company time. The meetings are planned and conducted by a designated leader who ideally is initially the immediate supervisor of the work group from which the members volunteered.

A trained, designated facilitator, who may also be the coordinator for the Quality Circle process at the location, coaches the leaders as they prepare for the weekly meetings, attends all meetings to provide assistance as needed and meets with the leaders following each meeting to provide reinforcement and constructive feedback.

The leaders and coordinator/facilitator, who have completed train-the-trainer classes prior to forming the Circles, conduct the initial training of the Circle members. The training consists of team building experiences and problem solving techniques, and generally requires the first five to seven one hour weekly Circle meetings.

Following their initial training, the Circle members select and solve work related problems by proceeding through the four numbered stages and one or two presentation stages of the systematic model for group problem solving shown in Figure 7-4. In general, the Circles follow the "steps" and utilize many of the "techniques" listed to the right of each stage of the model.

The two unnumbered stages of the model represent opportunities for Circle members to make presentations to appropriate representa-

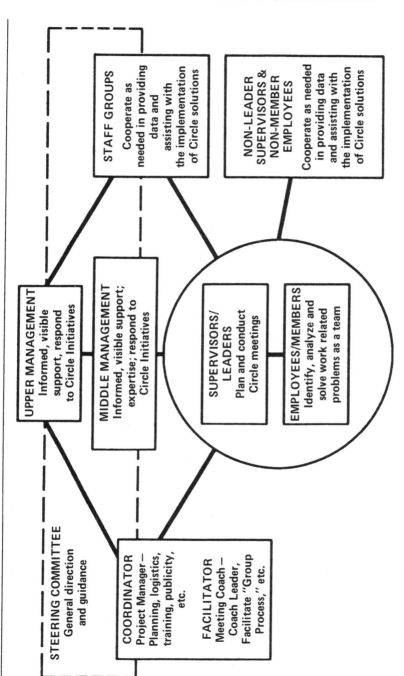

Figure 7-3. GTE Quality Circles—Roles.

Source: Daniel M. Falvey, *The Quality Circles Approach to Employee Involvement at GTE* (Stamford, Conn.: GTE Service Corporation, 1984).

Figure 7-4.   GTE Problem Solving.

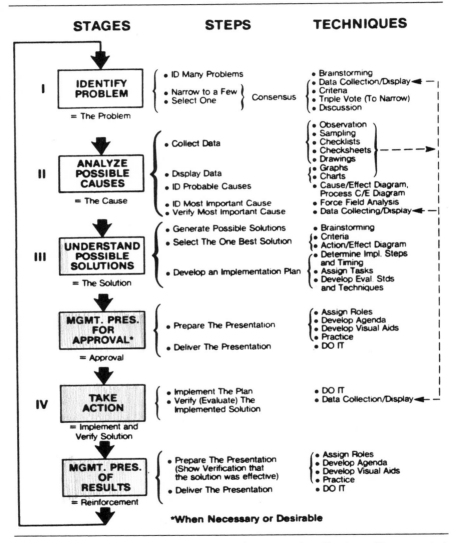

Source: Daniel M. Falvey, *The Quality Circles Approach to Employee Management at GTE* (Stamford, Conn.: GTE Service Corporation, 1984).

tives of management either for approval (if requested) or to present results (after the Circle's solution has been implemented and evaluated). These management presentations have the additional benefit of encouraging the two-way reinforcement between Circle members and management.

Generally speaking, the Circles choose to work on problems which have the greatest impact on their immediate work group. They typically use from three to seven of the "techniques" listed in Figure 7-4 to narrow down the problem, analyze the causes, generate potential solutions, then implement the most practical solution themselves, with the help of staff and other non-Circle members as needed.

Quality Circles clearly are *not* a "quick fix" for quality, productivity or attitude-related organizational ills. It is important for management and Circle leaders and members alike to have realistic expectations, especially during the first year or so of a Circle implementation when tangible results are generally modest. But, the evidence clearly supports Circles as a worthwhile approach to improving results in these and a number of other relevant areas as part of a well balanced strategy for organizational improvement at locations where sustained, long-term management commitment exists.

As an example, at GTE's Communication Systems plant in El Paso, Texas, employee involvement in quality circles projects has yielded a return on investment of 3.75:1 to the company. Quality Circles members feel their efforts have been worthwhile as well. GTE presented Quality Circles members with a questionnaire covering their attitudes to the Circles. At the El Paso plant, 98 percent of the members indicated that QC's should be continued and expanded. Furthermore, 93 percent of the respondents replied that the time spent in QC activities is well justified by improvements made in the organization's effectiveness.

On the whole, GTE Circles seem to be consistently cost effective. More than half of those locations which have tracked tangible-costed benefits have reported data indicating that the return on investment from implementing circles has been 3:1 or greater. Indeed, "Quality Circles have emerged as the single, most broadly-accepted and successful team problem-solving employee involvement option in use throughout the GTE Corporation."[18]

NOTES

1. *Insight* 9, no. 2 (1985): 8–9.
2. Ibid., 7.
3. Philip B. Crosby, *Quality without Tears: The Art of Hassle-Free Management* (New York: McGraw-Hill, 1984), 59.
4. Ibid., 66.
5. Ibid., 74.
6. Ibid., 85.
7. D. H. McPherson (Remarks made to the alumni of the Philip Crosby Institute, Winter Park, Florida, July 1, 1985).
8. "'Permanent Attitude Change' Sparks High Quality Productivity Gains at Florida Electric Utility," (Case study 39, American Productivity Center, September 1984), 2.
9. Internal Florida Power and Light Company publication, n.d., 2.
10. "Permanent Attitude Change," 3.
11. Internal Florida Power and Light publication, n.d., 11.
12. "Permanent Attitude Change," 1.
13. Internal Florida Power and Light publication, 6.
14. Ibid., 10.
15. "Permanent Attitude Change," 4.
16. Ibid., 6.
17. Ibid.
18. Daniel M. Falvey, *The Quality Circles Approach to Employee Involvement at GTE* (Stamford, Conn.: GTE Service Corporation, 1984), 16.

IV EMPLOYEE INVOLVEMENT AND MOTIVATION

8 FUNDAMENTALS OF EMPLOYEE INVOLVEMENT

Producing a quality product requires more than the implementation of a quality control process. Recurring throughout the preceding discussions is a constant theme—a company cannot implement the specific methods described without the enthusiastic cooperation of its work force. A carefully composed plan may succeed on paper only to molder unnoticed in the files of the unmotivated employee. It is crucial to involve each employee personally in the success of the plan. The traditional conflicts between management and the work force can destroy any chance of soliciting that essential commitment. It will not be enough for top-level management to issue the equivalent of a royal decree and sit back expecting immediate results. One could argue that anyone would prefer to contribute to the production of quality, but this will not automatically be the case if a worker feels that the only good being served is that of a company that does inspire his or her loyalty.

Perhaps the best way to show just how basic this process is, and how carefully a company must proceed in order to earn the commitment of its work force, is to take a look at how one organization set out to achieve its purpose. The following letter from N. P. Atherton, vice president of Spark Plug Manufacturing Operations at Champion Spark Plug Company, outlines their innovative program.

I am pleased to share with you the approaches that we have adopted at Champion Spark Plug Company to insure our continued commitment to our customers. We at Champion firmly believe that our quality has been, and will continue to be, a result of the combined effort of all our employees.

We initially embarked into a more in-depth form of participative management through our "TLC" or "Tender Loving Care" program. This program was started in 1983 by our Detroit, Michigan, Ceramic employees to express their concern for the careful handling of our spark plug insulators. This theme was expanded to cover many activities which include communications, teamwork, and employee involvement. In August 1983, our Training Department produced and presented to all our employees a videotape entitled "TLC & ME." This twenty-eight-minute production was narrated by our Detroit Ceramic employees to emphasize the importance of careful insulator handling. These employees explain the operations they perform [to] insure the shipment of a quality insulator to our assembly plants.

In November 1983, we began holding semiannual plant visitations and meetings with our employees. During these visits, top-management personnel are present to explain our current position, outline manufacturing improvements, and respond to questions from employees. These executives also tour the facilities and have face-to-face contact with the employees "on their turf." As a result of these visits, we have received hundreds of questions, comments, suggestions, and ideas which have proven very beneficial in achieving improvements in the operations and, certainly, morale.

A second videotape was produced and presented to all employees in January 1984. This presentation again utilized our employees, from all the domestic plants, to explain how they perform their jobs and the quality inspection required during the manufacture of a Champion spark plug.

In March 1984, we held a "Take Ten For TLC" meeting in each plant, where we shut down all domestic facilities for ten minutes and asked the employees to complete survey forms. This survey produced very positive feedback regarding all phases of our "TLC" program. This survey also indicated an employee interest in the development of an Employee Involvement Program.

In July, 1984, we formally introduced our Employee Involvement Program. A suggestion form is available to all employees should they desire to submit a comment, idea, or suggestion. Our employees selected the program name of "C.H.A.M.P.S.—Champion Hourly and Management Problem Solving." The program structure was organized, and three pilot teams were formed and put into operations in the Spring 1985. We presently have twenty teams operating in three of our plants. These teams allow the employees to meet, discuss, and collectively address things they would like to see improved, changed, or modified to improve their work environment, job satisfaction, or product quality. The Employee Involvement Program "TLC" is structured for the mutual benefit of all employees. Programs like these promote teamwork and improve communication, while fostering a sense of purpose and direction throughout the entire organization.

In September, 1985, we presented our third videotape to our employees. This tape, unlike the first two, was not narrated by our employees. The tape did, however, show many of our employees at work in our different manufacturing operations. The narration was directed at our employees, extending thanks to them for their efforts, commitment to quality and the pride they have directed toward our manufacturing efforts.

In the fall 1985, we began conducting monthly supervisor/employee meetings. These meetings are held in each department to keep our employees informed about departmental activities and to respond to questions and comments that they may have.

In January, 1986, we began conducting management meetings. Our top manufacturing executives meet with department supervisors and staff personnel to furnish them with information relative to total company operations.

As you can see, our "TLC" program has encompassed many different areas. We are continually working toward improved communications, reduce project implementation time, and afford our employees the opportunity to become more involved in the decisions affecting their operations.

We are presently in the formative stages of our Statistical Process Control program. We have done extensive research concerning S.P.C. to insure successful implementation. We are now conducting training for our employees to familiarize them with the benefits of an S.P.C. program. Along with personal training of our Quality Control Department, we have included the use of (6) tapes covering (40) topics concerning the S.P.C. program. These tapes will assist in the explanation and application of S.P.C. and enhance the implementation.

We are instituting an S.P.C. program to furnish our customers with a quality product. The program will also enable our employees to become more involved and satisfied with their work environment.[1]

The production of quality is hard work. It takes time to learn new systems, to get used to new work styles, to apply new methodologies. Rearrangement of the interpersonal structure of a company to allow the free exchange of ideas that is fundamental to quality control may be threatening to those accustomed to conventional lines of communication. No worker will be willing to adapt without the belief that the company is as committed to him or her as it is to its own success. The same holds true for suppliers. There is little incentive to respond to great demands for quality if there is no guarantee that such a response will be rewarded. Any American company that has decided to strive for improved quality must first work diligently to encourage in both workers and suppliers the degree of motivation necessary to achieve its goals.

LONG-TERM EMPLOYMENT

One effective way to prove to the worker that his or her contributions are taken seriously is to offer some measure of job security. Perhaps it is time to consider the radical idea that all classes of labor are entitled to long-term employment, except in unusual circumstances beyond a firm's control. Currently in this country, it is all too usual for companies to close individual plants when profits take a turn for the worse. Companies now have the luxury to hire and fire almost indiscriminately according to economic fluctuations and managerial whims. With such uncertainty ever present, it is unreasonable to expect unqualified support from the worker. How a company acts in these situations can have an enormous effect—good or ill—on company loyalty.

Take, for example, the diverging responses of Pitney Bowes and NCR to the crises induced by computer technology. Both companies dominate their particular industries, one in postage meters the other in cash registers. Both firms recognized the need to make the change from electromechanics to electronics a few years ago. They both undertook massive engineering and manufacturing conversions.

NCR, according to Pitney Bowes, made a common and economic acceptable business decision. Instead of updating their Dayton, Ohio, plants by an expensive retooling program, which would have necessitated the retraining of all their production workers, they decided to close the plants, building new ones in the Southwest. New people were hired and trained, while thousands of assembly-line workers in Dayton lost their jobs. Pitney Bowes chose a different route, setting up a special training center in Stamford to retrain their electromechanical employees as electronic assembly workers. The program resulted in an upgraded plant without a single production worker losing his or her job. Two different approaches to a similar problem—both having their pluses and minuses depending upon the criteria used.

Pitney Bowes attempts to maintain a small-company, family atmosphere—everyone, including the president, is on a first-name basis. Since 1942, it has relied on its "Council of Personnel Relations" to handle personnel problems. The Council tries to echo the actual structure of the organization by including equal numbers of managers and workers, both elected by their peers. Other mechanisms in use are a suggestion system that allows an employee to earn up to $50,000 for an accepted idea, a preretirement education program, no mandatory retirement age (contrary to the Japanese system of forced retirement at 55 to 60 years of age), a generous benefits package, and a profit-sharing plan, in place since 1940. Open communication is fostered through a formal "Annual Jobholder's Meeting," intended to give employees an accounting of the business and a forum for discussion of their problems.

In effect, Pitney Bowes operates its own version of a Nenko system, although it appears to have no Japanese roots. With such a history of commitment to the welfare of its workforce, it was almost inevitable that Pitney Bowes would face the challenge of the new technology in the manner it did.[2]

Springs Industries, Inc., a manufacturer of bed linens and towels, has a similar commitment to job security. Roughly 20 percent of their employees have been with the company for twenty-five years or longer, some ranging up to fifty years. In the last three years, the firm has been forced to close three of its plants due to competitive conditions. However, they delayed the closings for periods of over six months in order to phase in the expansion of other nearby plants. Nearly all of the displaced employees from two of the closing plants were moved and retained. In the third, more than two-thirds of the workers were moved to a nearby expanded plant and their employment continued.

It is unlikely that extensive management of employees' social and cultural activities will ever have a place in American industry. Yet some degree of involvement is recommended, if only to demonstrate to workers that they are recognized as more than just part of the company's physical plant. Springs Industries has a foundation, begun nearly fifty years ago, that is chartered to provide educational, recreational, and cultural activities for the communities in which its plants are located. As an example, they have run the largest nonjuried art show in the Southeast for the past twenty-seven years.[3]

Long-term employment carries with it the need for extensive employee training, to ensure a motivated work force that is loyal, competent, and flexible. Obviously this type of training is not only time consuming but very expensive. However, if an employee is expected to remain with a company for many years, the cost of training, amortized over the period of employment, becomes relatively low. The employee also realizes that if the greater part of his or her work life is going to be spent in the same company, is only sensibly self-interested to perform at a satisfactory productivity level in order to help guarantee the organization's prosperity. Free of the fears that normally exist in a competitive workplace, workers begin to function at levels of efficiency unusual in the traditional system.

COMMUNICATION AND TEAMWORK

If a prerequisite to quality is communication, then it is, of course, important to eliminate as far as possible the tensions that can exist among the various levels and kinds of workers. If hourly and salaried employees are working together, efforts must be made to improve working conditions for all concerned. It will do a company little good to elicit the support of its salaried workers if those paid by the hour are left out in the cold. The reverse is equally true. At Mohasco Corporation, a major manufacturer of carpets and furniture, for example, entrance into its new program is limited to its hourly employees. Supervisory personnel have reacted negatively because they feel that top management has provided more training and attention to their subordinates than to them.[4] Many corporations, in fact, choose to avoid this problem by putting all of their employees on salary, which can go a long way toward crumbling some of those vertical barriers.

It can safely be said that most companies with established employee involvement programs believe that unions are almost superfluous in their organizations. However, where union and nonunion workers are present, they must be treated equitably. The potential for conflict here is great, especially if the company's payment structure favors one group over the other. If, for instance, a profit-sharing plan is closed to union members, they may feel some resentment, even if they are receiving higher base wages. Still, there is evidence that, at the very least, a new commitment to the work force can greatly reduce the overall number and intensity of union-management disagreements.

Pay equity is not the only factor to consider. It is equally essential that management actively acknowledges the value of workers at all levels of the organization. Even in companies that are experiencing extreme difficulties, such as the LTV Steel Company, which is presently fighting for survival and seeking relief under Chapter 11 of the bankruptcy laws, teamwork has become important. In an internal publication the company's policy is clearly stated:

> People are working to their full capacity in an environment that recognizes and rewards their full potential as individuals. In 1981, in a joint effort with the United Steelworkers of America, Labor Management Participating Teams (LMPTs) were initiated on an experimental basis and today this process has become a keystone of LTV Steel's relationship with the United Steel Workers of America at 13 locations throughout the organization. This concept is destined to play an integral part in LTV Steel's approach to involving the entire work force in finding imaginative solutions to the demanding problems faced in the ever increasing competitive world of this decade.

The LTV process calls for an end to the adversary relationship, recognizing that workers on the shop floor have the greatest expertise in identifying and solving problems. Support for the program comes from key management and union officials, with credit for development and growth going to both union leadership and local management. The process includes the creation of joint problem-solving teams, composed of hourly and salaried employees who are extensively trained in communications, group interactive skills, problem-solving skills, statistics, data gathering, and a consensus-approach to group decisionmaking.[5]

Teamwork in action was evident during our visit to the Ford Motor Company's Lincoln division in Dearborn, Michigan. A salaried manager and a union member work together as a problem-solving team on the factory floor. They have the right to address any non-contract-related problem. One could sense a group dynamic forming in this company, where labor and management are on a first-name basis, and the old adversary relationship between labor and management seems at least to be moderated.

Top management must be willing to decentralize decisionmaking to even lower levels in the hierarchy than exist at the present time. Indirect control can still be maintained through the use of sophisticated management information systems, which will ensure that any decisions made by middle management that are not congruent with the needs of the firm can be altered in a timely fashion. Decisionmaking should really be a companywide affair; everyone affected should have the opportunity to get involved. Although this is time-consuming, the acceptance and successful implementation of a decision will be far more likely than if it is made unilaterally. Executives will, of course, continue to have major decisionmaking roles in their corporations. Decisions that would effect the entire organization and require detailed information beyond the scope of middle management would be reserved for top management and its teams.

Other personnel steps to insure an individual's dignity in the workplace should be evaluated and implemented—time clocks should be phased out, for instance, and their use limited to disciplinary requirements. It is degrading to have to punch in and out of a plant. It is the same as being told you are not trusted to give a full day's work. Without trust, we are trapped in the old adversary mode of workers versus management. To create a unified environment, distinctions between work levels should be eliminated or at least minimized. Standardized work uniforms, such as those worn in a Japanese factory, may not be necessary, but perhaps the time for "perks," such as executive dining rooms, executive parking spaces, and overly plush offices, is past. Black and Decker, manufacturers of small electric hand tools, has applied many of these innovations and has motivated its managers and workers to work together as a team. The results has been the company's ability to bring out new products in a timely manner at attractive prices in a highly competitive market.[6]

JAPANESE COMPANIES IN AMERICA

Clearly, the development of an employee involvement program is not straightforward. There is no way to arrive at a cut-and-dried plan to motivate all the employees in American industry. Employee involvement is the product of a complete alteration of the attitudes of everyone in an organization. The means to this transformation will differ as drastically as the personalities of the people involved. Perhaps the stories of three Japanese automobile companies that have set up operations in the United States will best serve to illustrate the various ways employee motivation can be achieved. These companies, and others like them, have thus far been quite successful in transplanting their management systems, appropriately modified, to the United States.

Honda of America

Back in 1959, when the American market for motorcycles was stagnating, Honda decided the time was ripe to enter the United States through the establishment of a sales office, American Honda. Only 160 motorcycles were sold during their first year in business, but Honda was determined to succeed.

The Boston Consulting Group's study, *Strategy Alternatives for the British Motorcycle Industry*, described Honda's strategy.[7] By 1960, Japanese motorcycle manufacturers had a decade of developing huge production volumes of small motorcycles in their domestic market behind them. Only 4 percent of motorcycle production was then exported, but large economies in the production of small motorcycles had already been achieved. As a result, volume-related cost reductions placed Japanese motorcycle manufacturers in a highly competitive position. Honda used this position to its advantage and started to market its small motorcycles in the United States.

For Americans living in the early 1960s, though, the motorcycle brought to mind images of the rough and rowdy Hell's Angels. Honda decided to change all that. Advertisements saying "You meet the nicest people on a Honda" and a retail price of under $250 (compared to $1000 to $1500 for the larger American and British motorcycles) soon swept Americans off their feet and onto a Honda. By 1964, nearly half of the motorcycles sold in the United States were Hondas. American Honda's sales soared from $500,000 in 1960 to $77 million in 1965, and Honda was producing hundreds of thousands of units a year in a once-dormant market.

Nine years later, in 1974, Honda commenced plans to build manufacturing facilities in the United States, in keeping with its policy of setting up plants in countries where its products are marketed. On September 10, 1979, the first Honda motorcycle built in America rolled off the production line in Marysville, Ohio. Today, approximately 60,000 motorcycles are produced every year in the Marysville plant.

Honda's success in the American motorcycle market has led to automobile production in the United States. The company's automobile manufacturing plant in Marysville now produces about 150,000 Accords a year. Workers are cross-trained to rotate jobs and can quickly shift production from one model to another whenever necessary. Retooling for new models can also be performed rapidly—within just a few minutes, Honda workers can change the shapes of doors or fenders.

In addition to parts shipped from Japan, Honda purchases parts from local suppliers, with whom it establishes long-term relationships in order to maintain just-in-time purchasing. Shipments from key suppliers are delivered by a dedicated carrier contracted to meet Honda's schedule. Honda shies away from using common carriers who deliver at their own convenience, since the company's just-in-time production is planned around on-time deliveries. Most of the plant's inventory consists of only several hours' worth of supplies.

When Shoichiro Irimajiri, president of Honda of America, moved from the Suzuka Factory in Japan in mid-1984 to assume responsibility for operations in Ohio, he left behind a factory where the average employee had seven and a half years' experience in manufacturing automobiles. Arriving at the Ohio plant, he found that the average American auto worker had less than one year's experience. Whether Honda would be successful in applying its approach to manufacturing automobiles in the U.S. was an uncertainty. Honda soon discovered it was not a problem at all.

In January 1985, *Car and Driver* magazine stated: "There is nothing wrong with a Honda Accord. Nothing. How many other cars can one say that about?" And, in December of 1985, *Consumer Reports* rated the quality of the Honda built in Ohio as high as those imported from Japan. According to company executives, the Accords produced at the Marysville plant are manufactured at roughly the same cost as those built by the parent company in Japan.

Honda's success in America can be attributed to an emphasis on cooperative labor relations. Rejecting traditional American management practices, by which workers have been treated like machines, Honda has transplanted the Japanese philosophy of treating employees as the company's most valuable asset. Competing through quality the Honda way begins with the recognition that human potential is limitless and the creation of a safe working environment that fosters creativity, involvement, and pride. Five principles underscore management's policy:

1. Proceed always with ambition and youthfulness.
2. Respect sound theory, develop fresh ideas, and make the most effective use of time.

3. Enjoy your work and always brighten your work atmosphere.
4. Strive constantly for a harmonious flow of work.
5. Be ever-mindful of the value of research and endeavor.

The atmosphere at Honda's Ohio plant exudes an aura of equality. Everyone who works there is known as an associate. Distinctions between management and labor are so blurred that one would be hard put to figure out who's who. Everyone wears the same white uniform. Everyone parks in the same parking lot, where there are no reserved spaces. Everyone eats in the same cafeterias. And everyone shares the same desks. Even the desk of President Shoichiro Irimajiri is in the same large room as a hundred other workers, with no walls to surround him.

At Honda, everyone is encouraged to improve upon existing practices. The whole approach to quality is based upon respect for the individual's intelligence. Quality is not mandated by placing quality inspectors at each step of the manufacturing process. Instead, each associate is trained to take pride in and be responsible for the quality of Honda's products.

Should a problem arise, management goes to the shop floor and asks the associates for their solutions. Honda has a saying that there is more knowledge on the factory floor than there is in the office. They have found from experience that the associate most directly involved is often the one best qualified to solve problems and improve the quality and process of production. Irimajiri elaborates:

> In order to make this reliance on our Associates succeed, our Associates have to understand our commitment to continuous improvement. We have to eliminate the fear of making and reporting mistakes. False pride that seeks to hide problems is one of the greatest barriers to quality. We encourage our Associates to tell of problems in their areas and then to apply their creativity to solving them.[8]

To date, the Ohio plant has remained nonunionized. Honda associates earn on average $11 per hour, slightly less than the $13 or $14 hourly wages that unionized workers make at GM or Ford. Even so, Honda's company benefits, training, and working conditions seem to compensate for this, and attempts to unionize the plant have yet to be successful. Receiving $2000 bonus checks and responses to aired grievances within two days probably tend to make many Honda workers wonder what good a union could possibly do.

Toyota Motor Company

In Fremont, California, General Motors operates a joint venture with Toyota known as New United Motor Manufacturing, Inc. (NUMMI). The Japanese, who are managing the plant according to Toyota's production system principles, have shaken up the American automobile industry. Chevrolet Novas (facsimiles of Toyota Corollas) have been rolling off the plant's assembly line since January 1986 with such efficiency that General Motors' executives are stunned. The Fremont plant, using UAW workers, is producing the Nova at a cost very close to the landed cost of the Corolla made in Japan— about $2500 less than similar automobiles produced in Detroit. While the Chevrolet Cavalier, the GM model comparable to the Nova, takes thirty-eight man-hours to produce, the Nova takes only twenty-one. None of this is at the expense of quality, either: In February 1986, *Consumer Reports* rated the Nova equal to or better than the Toyota Corolla.

Four years ago, before the start of GM's venture with Toyota, General Motors' Fremont auto-assembly plant was in a sorry state. Production was interrupted by frequent wildcat strikes and raging labor-management disputes. Absenteeism levels of 20 percent, along with an average of 5,000 outstanding grievances—averaging one for each employee—hardly suggested that workers were satisfied with their jobs. In 1982, General Motors decided to close the plant.

Within a matter of months after the Japanese reopened Fremont's doors, the plant was completely turned around. Toyota rehired most of the UAW workers, including their militant leaders, and organized them into cross-trained work teams. Job classifications are kept to a minimum, as is management—there are only five layers in the new company's organizational structure.

Productivity has increased dramatically. Today, NUMMI's 2,500 workers can assemble 240,000 cars a year. When GM operated the plant, it required 5,000 or more workers to produce an equivalent amount. Unlike Nissan and Honda, who have started operations in the United States with nonunionized, less expensive labor, Toyota is working successfully with a union accustomed to being management's adversary. Absentee levels have been under 2 percent, and there are only two grievances outstanding. NUMMI's UAW representative, Joel D. Smith, explained in *Business Week* (1986): "We have the same members, the same building, the same technology—just different management and a different production system."[9]

The plant is outdated—since the Japanese didn't add much new technology—yet productivity at Fremont exceeds that of most of GM's new, highly automated plants. Experts agree that the emphasis the Toyota management style places upon employee involvement in decisionmaking, thorough training, and lean layers of middle management is responsible. General Motors is learning from Fremont that high-tech plants won't make high grades without good management.

Toyota management installed a just-in-time system and a flexible assembly line handled by teams of workers who take charge of their own jobs. There are no industrial engineers to tell them how to perform—they've become their own efficiency experts. When, for example, the plant was operated by GM, the worker who installed windows on right front doors had to make three trips from his toolbox to each car as it moved along the assembly line. Nobody bothered to ask him if he could come up with a faster way of installing the windows. Under Toyota management, a faster way has been found. By simply rearranging the equipment, the window installer only needs to walk to each car once. The job used to require twenty-three steps in the old days; it now takes only eleven.

Toyota wants its workers to feel like equals. At NUMMI, executive parking spaces are nonexistent. And inside the spotlessly clean plant, where every part and tool is kept within easy reach, there's no office for the foreman, who instead sits at a small table with a couple of chairs in an open space right on the line. In addition, management has pledged to cut their own salaries before workers are asked to make temporary concessions, such as accepting layoffs, salary reductions, or paybacks, during bad times.

Toyota has managed to win over the once-belligerent UAW workers by earning their trust and treating them with dignity and respect. Changes in labor-management relations haven't been less than startling. President of the old GM local, Tony DeJesus, led a wildcat strike in 1978. Today he's president of the new UAW local at NUMMI. In *Business Week*, he remarked: "When GM was here, we hated each other. It's true we were partly to blame. There were a lot of drugs and a lot of absenteeism. But we were a reflection of the SOBs we worked for. Now management's given us a voice and more responsibility and listens to us."[10]

Nissan Motor Corporation

The Nissan Motor Corporation in U.S.A., the American subsidiary of Nissan Ltd. in Japan, has put up $64 million to train new workers for its truck plant in Smyrna, Tennessee. Getting hired by Nissan is not easy—one employee by the name of Espinoza, a Mexican-American who came to Nissan from Chicago, was interviewed several times over a six-month period and was required to undergo extra training before becoming employed as a paint-maintenance technician. Once hired, however, Nissan workers are employed for life.

Extensive training awaits all new employees. To train for his job of maintaining an automated paint booth, Espinoza followed a personalized program that included 120 hours of electronics instruction, 120 hours of machine-shop training, 60 hours of hydraulics, and another 60 hours of welding. Nissan even sent him to Japan to learn about the entire manufacturing process. In their view, the more an employee understands the whole picture, the better he or she will perform a specific job.

Nissan operates with only five levels of management. Having come from Ford, which operated with twelve management levels during his tenure there, President Marvin Runyon argues that Nissan's loose managerial structure helps communication flow more easily throughout the company.

All employees, salaried and hourly alike, work together and participate in any decisionmaking that affects their jobs. According to Espinoza, "no one draws a line between workers and managers here. Everyone is treated with respect. Even the janitor is likely to have lunch with the plant manager and offer his advice on maintenance. The plant manager will listen, and take notes."

Nissan's family-team approach places tremendous stress on doing the best possible job. Quality Circles consisting of small groups of employees from all levels meet periodically throughout the day to tackle problems. Anyone who detects a defect in a vehicle is encouraged to stop the assembly line and have it corrected.

Nissan believes that their management style promotes an individual pride in workmanship and a team pride in quality—attitudes that enable ordinary workers to achieve extraordinary things.

These three examples offer ample proof that so-called Japanese management techniques can work in this country. If the Japanese can tailor their methods to suit their American workers, how much more certain, then, that American managers, when determined to arouse in their employees and suppliers their indispensable commitment to company goals, will be able to fashion appropriate programs. In the following chapter, case studies detailing what five American companies have done will, we feel, successfully demonstrate that this assurance is justified.

NOTES

1. N. P. Atherton, vice president, Spark Plug Manufacturing Operations, Champion Spark Plug Company, Toledo, Ohio, letter to authors, February 5, 1986.

2. Thomas F. McGarry, vice president of corporate communications, Pitney Bowes, Stamford, Conn., letter to authors, December 11, 1985.

3. J. Marshall Doswell, vice president of corporate communications, Springs Industries, Inc., Fort Mills, S.C., letter to authors, February 21, 1986.

4. Joseph P. Lamb, vice president of human resources, Mohasco Corporation, Amsterdam, N.Y., letter to authors, January 22, 1986.

5. Internal LTV Steel Company publication entitled "Labor Management Participation Teams," n.d.

6. Yoshi Tsurumi, "Management Adaptability, Not Open Markets, Will End U.S. Trade Deficit," *The Japan Economic Journal* (March 8, 1986): 7.

7. Boston Consulting Group, *Strategy Alternatives the British Motorcycle Industry* (London, England: Her Majesty's Stationery Office, July 30, 1975).

8. Shoichiro Irimajiri, "Honda's Approach to a Mature Industry," (Speech at the fifth conference of the U.S.-Japan Automotive Industry, "Entrepreneurship in a Mature Industry," Ann Arbor, Michigan, March 5, 1985).

9. Aaron Bernstein, et al., "The Difference Japanese Management Makes," *Business Week*, July 14, 1986, 47.

10. Ibid., 49.

9 CASES IN EMPLOYEE MOTIVATION

WORTHINGTON INDUSTRIES

Worthington Industries, a manufacturer of steel products based in Columbus, Ohio, has fared quite well in an industry where others have done poorly. with total sales of $701 million in fiscal 1985, and sales and earnings growth rates of 22.7 percent and 21.8 percent, respectively, over the past ten years. Worthington Industries has also been proclaimed one of the hundred best companies to work for in America by authors Levering, Moskowitz, and Katz.

When John McConnell, chairman and CEO of Worthington Industries, is asked the secret of his company's success, he mentions shrewd diversification, innovation, and dedication to product quality, customer service, and technical expertise. But, above all, he stresses good human relations.

McConnell believes in concentrating on three basics: "Number one, you have to motivate people. After you motivate them you have to constantly communicate with them. And then you have to recognize their efforts, give them a pat on the back in various ways."[1]

According to McConnell, motivating people at Worthington is simple:

We happen to believe that the people in our company are the most important asset we have, and so we treat them that way. This means every employee,

171

from the bottom all the way to the top. We don't care where they work, they are important. We do not have the 'us and them' attitude. Our employees have one objective in mind, to make a profit for Worthington. They know what profit is because we have taught them.[2]

They also know what profit is because Worthington shares it with them in abundance. Sixteen percent of the company's pretax profits is paid out to the firm's nonunionized employees (about 60 percent of the total work force) on a quarterly basis. During the past few years, production employees have received quarterly bonus checks averaging $3000. Up to 50 percent of their annual compensation may be paid through the profit-sharing plan. Management receives an average of 60 percent of their total compensation in bonuses. Most companies do not base such a high percentage of an executive's compensation on corporate earnings, but McConnell feels that "management people should not be hired hands, . . . it is important for them to be accountable for a company's profitability and be compensated according to the performance of the company they're running."

Both management and production employees are salaried; nobody works on an hourly basis. Profits are doled out to employees based on their individual annual salaries, so the incentive is great to become more productive and improve one's position within the company.

Worthington also has a deferred profit-sharing plan to provide for their employees' long-term security. A portion of the company's pretax earnings is placed in the deferred plan twice a year. Employees with the company three years become 30 percent vested. Each year thereafter they earn an additional 10-percent share.

According to McConnell, "the most important thing you have to do with employees, especially when you have a profit-sharing plan, is communicate with them. An incentive plan will not be effective if all your employees don't believe in it." Worthington employees feel comfortable approaching management with questions. Supervisors are encouraged to be available, and McConnell himself tries to be in the Columbus plants twice a week to answer questions or listen to complaints.

Employee councils have been established in most of Worthington's plants. Composed of production workers selected by their peers to serve two-year terms, the councils are kept up to date by management on business developments and problem areas that need improvement. They also present to management any questions, suggestions, and grievances from the employees. The results of these discussions are reported to the employees. McConnell states that "this is an excellent communication tool because some people will never feel comfortable speaking with management no matter what you do to encourage them, but they will open up to their peers. This way we receive input from many more employees."

Worthington conducts periodic seminars to ensure that everyone understands his or her role in the profit-sharing plan. Employees are guided step by step through a profit-and-loss statement and shown how profits are generated only after such items as cost of goods sold and operating expenses have been accounted for. Employees learn how they can help curb expenses by reducing the costs over which they have control, such as scrap rate (there are no quality inspectors at Worthington; the workers themselves are responsible for quality), absenteeism, rejection rates, and equipment and supplies usage. The seminar leader will conduct various exercises to show how increased profits can arise from controlling these costs. Given this chance to increase the size of their bonus checks, Worthington's employees respond with enthusiasm: the rejection rate is only 1 percent, well below the industry average of 4 percent, and absenteeism is a mere 2 percent.

Recognition completes the triad of management concepts at Worthington. Promotions are according to merit, rather than seniority. Management maintains that the Japanese system of promoting by seniority ignores the efforts of those who work the hardest and produce the most.

Service and attendance awards are presented at annual employee banquets held for each division. Employees who miss less than four hours of work per year are rewarded with six shares of company stock; those who miss between four to eight hours receive four shares. One man in Louisville, who hasn't missed a day in seven years, has accumulated shares now worth over $8,000.

Production records are posted on each machine. Workers who set records are given gifts. Worthington believes that such indications of approval are a small price to pay for the motivation they generate.

Employee turnover is very low at Worthington—less than 2 percent. During recessionary periods, the company avoids layoffs by assigning workers to new jobs such as equipment maintenance and painting. Nor do the employees have much desire to leave. Once they receive their first bonus after being with the company for three months, they're pretty much sold.

Unions have made little progress at the plants. When McConnell founded Worthington in 1955, he was determined not to have unions: "I have no ill feelings toward them, however I've always believed that management organizes unions, unions do not organize unions. If you run your operations properly and if you are fair, honest, straightforward and keep your people informed, your employees will not want to be represented by an outside party." Worthington has acquired several facilities where unions were already established, but none of the original plants has ever become unionized. In fact, when the workers at the Baltimore, Chicago, and Puerto Rico plants found out about the profit-sharing plan, which is not open to union employees, they voted to decertify their unions—hardly a big surprise, considering that otherwise they would miss out on an average of $12,000 a year in bonuses.

For four consecutive years, *Forbes* has ranked Worthington Industries number one in profitability and growth within the industry. McConnell has no plans to slow down the momentum. Favoring those acquisitions that increase the company's share in existing markets and provide geographical expansion for existing products, he insists that they've only scratched the surface.

GENERAL MOTORS

In 1984, General Motors and the United Auto Workers negotiated a labor contract designed to benefit both parties. Roger Smith, chairman of General Motors, regards the new agreement as the first move toward a partnership to manage change.

One of the most significant developments that arose from the negotiations is a new job security agreement—Job Opportunity Bank-Security (JOB-S). General Motors has committed up to $1 billion for this program, which will continue for six years. The JOB-S program guarantees that no GM employee with one or more years of seniority will be laid off for any of the following reasons: the introduction of new technology; outsourcing; negotiated productivity improvements; or transfers or consolidations of work resulting in less work content.

Any employees whose jobs are eliminated for one of these reasons will be retrained (to refine their present skills or learn new ones), used as replacements to help train other workers, provided with new jobs if openings arise, or given nontraditional assignments outside of their bargaining units. A JOB-S committee, composed of the plant managers, other representatives of management, and the local shop committee will jointly administer the program at each plant and decide how to place redundant employees, with reference to the needs of both the business and the individuals affected. Management no longer retains the sole power to make these decisions, as was the case in the past.

General Motors believes that the JOB-S program will bring about changes in employees' attitudes. Because no one will be laid off as a result of the introduction of new technology, employees will no longer resist productivity improvements. Robots will be welcomed, for the employee who is replaced by one will be retrained for a more interesting and satisfying job. Roger Smith is "confident that employees who are no longer concerned about losing their jobs will themselves come forward with suggestions for improving operational effectiveness." He mentions the case of a woman worker at GM's Pontiac engine plant: automation replaced her strenuous job as an assembler, providing her with the opportunity to supervise the robots operating three lines. She told Smith she loves the work. And the parts that are now assembled by robots and checked by machine vision are 100 percent perfect, all the time.

Another joint management/labor program—the Joint Growth and Opportunity Committee has been set up at GM. This "Go Committee" looks for new ways to employ workers displaced by productivity improvements, studying opportunities outside of GM's traditional car, truck, and diesel engine business. General Motors' nontraditional business areas include robotics (the company now operates a joint venture with Fanuc of Japan to produce industrial robots in the United States), data processing, and machine intelligence.

Incentives have been built into the contract to promote attendance. Smith explains how the new bonus program works: "Starting with the 1985 calendar year, employees will receive a $50 attendance-recognition award for every quarter in which they have perfect attendance. A full year of perfect attendance will earn the employee an additional $300 award, for a total of $500 for the year. Three out of four perfect quarters of attendance will earn the employee an additional $150, for a yearly total of $300." In addition, profit-sharing will continue at GM, and the Guaranteed Income Stream—a payment plan for long-seniority employees who are laid off—will be maintained.

General Motors hopes to end the adversarial management/labor relations that have deterred progress in the past. In his 1984 speech to the Management Research Center at the University of Wisconsin at Milwaukee, Smith summed up GM's new approach to labor relations:

> Our employees increasingly are a fixed asset to Motors—not a variable cost. We are moving away from the concept that we buy our employees' services only when we need them to make our products. As all good business people know, it's important to maximize your return on a fixed asset. And in the case of employees, I think the way to do that is develop a real working part-nership. American industry is beginning to realize that a stable, well-trained work force will help achieve higher quality and productivity.
>
> . . . Business—hoping to do well in an increasingly competitive market-place—must be equally sensitive today to the needs of these employees. A company can't be effective in the workplace without its employees, total involvement and commitment—and business knows it.
>
> Both sides have had a pretty narrow provincial orientation in the past. And their attitudes too often have been adversarial. But the pressures of world-wide competition have hit both squarely on the head and greatly broadened their view.
>
> It's a good thing. They'll do a better job. And all of us—companies, unions, employees, customers, and the country—will be vastly better off for this more enlightened, more united approach.[3]

General Motors recognizes the value of teamwork in successfully managing change. On May 9, 1985, GM held a groundbreaking cere-mony for its new UAW/GM Human Resource Center in Michigan. "Just as Saturn marked the commitment of General Motors and the UAW to make a competitive new *car* in a new way, so will this center mark our mutual resolve to deal with *people* in a new way," says Smith.[4]

GM's new human-relations approach places more priority on people than on machines. GM recognizes that skill development and training in the use of new processes and equipment is necessary for employees to understand the high technology that is penetrating their workplace. The paperless plants of the future, run by automation and linked by computer communications, will require a well-trained work force schooled in the essentials of human relations, problem-solving, and process control. Employees at the company's new assembly plant in Orion township were sent to classes for as long as six months before producing their first car. At the new Detroit-Hamtramk Assembly Center, GM has invested in a million man-hours of training. And at GM's future factory in Saginaw, skilled tradesmen will receive special training up to a full year.

Managing change requires a new spirit of entrepreneurship—enthusiasm, creativity, and willingness to take risks—especially in a mature industry characterized by an aversion to new technologies, saturated markets, and conservative, complacent bureaucrats. New ideas must flow and experiments must be made. General Motors is planning on unleashing this new spirit.

In his speech to the U.S.-Japan Auto Conference in 1985, F. James McDonald, president of General Motors, sketched out the principles of GM's philosophy of entrepreneurship: [5]

Centralized policy making with decentralized control.

Given the peculiar scope and complexity of our business, top management must encourage innovation—but without abdicating responsibility. Decentralized control is the answer.

Inherent in this principle is the need to move decisionmaking as far down as possible to allow people more freedom of operation. Participative management is essential to the company's health, but management cannot tell its employees how to bring it about. Quality ethics are established by management for all of GM, but each plant and each division must decide for itself how to reach those objectives.

Everyone is a potential innovator.

The plain fact is that everybody is an expert on how to do his or her job. No employee wants to produce defects. Given the proper environment, a free flow of ideas, suggestions, and contributions to quality will come forth.

Potential innovators receive ideas from one another. This is why GM promotes simultaneous engineering—people brought together from design, engineering, toolmaking, manufacturing, and assembly—to contribute collectively to attaining the optimum in high quality and customer satisfaction with a minimum of costs.

Invest, then give people the freedom to achieve.

That's what we've done with our high-tech venture—with GMF Robotics, EDS, and the various machine-intelligence companies we've invested in over the last year or two. . . . In all of our high-tech ventures, we hope to fan the sparks of entrepreneurialism into a roaring blaze of new applications.

General Motors has mapped out a new competitive strategy to encourage the spirit of entrepreneurlism. The company will be internally reorganized to cut out bureaucracy and redundancy and make it more responsive to the changing needs of its customers. And further commitments will be made to improve labor relations, as well as to promote advances in new technology and people-oriented systems.

FORD MOTOR COMPANY

Ford's new Taurus and its companion car, the Mercury Sable, represent a complete turnaround in American automobile manufacturing. Back in 1980, an idea was born: The Ford Motor Company would compete against the Japanese by beating them at their own game. With a $3 billion investment in the Taurus-Sable project, quality as their top priority, and some know-how from the Japanese, Ford was off to a new start.

The initial step was to modify Ford's organizational structure, unifying work efforts between departments. Traditionally, product planners, designers, engineers, manufacturing, and suppliers worked in sequence over a five-year period to develop a new automobile. This structure had its flaws: each unit was isolated from the other, communication between them was poor, and building a car was broken into a series of segmented steps for which no one bore the overall responsibility.

Borrowing from the Japanese, Ford built the concept of teamwork into the new structure through the establishment of "Team Taurus." "Program Management"—representatives from planning, design, engineering, and manufacturing working together as a group—was the new approach Team Taurus would take. Because Team Taurus was closely involved in all aspects of production from the very start, the team was able to solve problems as soon as they arose, before they reached crisis levels. For instance, suggestions for design changes that resulted in higher productivity or better quality were being offered by people in manufacturing. In the past, it was uncommon for manufacturing people to have much say in the way Ford's cars were designed.

Workers were having their say as well—a major divergence from the way American automobile manufacturers have commonly managed production. Before the car entered the design stage, Ford asked its production employees for their ideas about ways to improve productivity. Many of the suggestions that poured in were quite useful. In one case, several workers complained that the body panels they had to handle consisted of too many pieces. Installing car doors was difficult, since the body panels were formed of up to eight pieces to a side. Management relayed the problem to design, who reduced the number of pieces per panel to only two. Another employee suggested that all bolts should have the same size head. His gripe was that workers had to struggle with too many different wrenches in the past. Ford took notes and implemented the change.

Such consultations between management and labor used to be unheard of in Detroit. None of the top honchos would have ever dreamed that production workers could provide helpful hints in designing an automobile. As Ford executive John A. Manoogian put it to reporter Russell Mitchell: "In the past we hired people for their arms and their legs. But we weren't smart enough to make use of their brains."[6]

Ford also decided to use the best-designed and -engineered automobiles in the world as models for their new car. For the first time, Ford did some of the "reverse engineering" that the Japanese habitually use to improve their products. They bought over fifty midsize cars and tore them apart piece by piece to study how they were designed and assembled, with the intention of either copying the best features these autos had to offer or making them better. When finished, Ford identified 400 "best-in-class" features, including the Toyota Supra's fuel-gauge accuracy and the accelerator-pedal feel on the Audi 5000. According to Ford executives, their Taurus-Sable meets or exceeds 80 percent of these 400 features.

The company's vendors have also had more input than ever before. In the past, it was common for Ford buyers to present vendors with parts specifications after the design was completely planned. Those who could offer the least expensive sources of supply were chosen— a precarious victory, since they always risked losing the business to any other vendor who could produce the same part for less. With Team Taurus in operation, however, traditional purchasing procedures went by the wayside. Before the design was planned, Ford's suppliers were receiving long-term contracts not only to provide supplies, but to become involved in product planning as well. Lewis Veraldi, head of the Taurus-Sable program, told *Business Week* reporter Mitchell: "We never had the supplier input we had on this car. Now we'll never do it any other way."[7]

To date, Ford's Taurus-Sable project seems to be paying off quite nicely. Over 130,000 deliveries were made by June 1986, with backlogged orders for 100,000 more. Many dealers even have customers willing to wait two whole months for a new Taurus or Sable.

Ford seems sold on adapting Japanese manufacturing concepts. Because they've found Team Taurus to be so successful in applying these concepts, they've labelled the Taurus-Sable project as a model of efficiency for all future programs. In May of 1986, the company decided to apply management by teamwork throughout the entire Ford corporation. Teamwork, they've discovered, really does help when it comes to producing a high-quality automobile.

MONSANTO

In 1985, the Monsanto Polymer Products Company (MPP) pushed Total Quality to the forefront of its business strategies. Monsanto's credo, "the best have the competitive edge," underscores its commitment to companywide efforts in quality control. Total quality, at Monsanto, means freedom from avoidable surprises, deviations, rework, and hassle, achieved by prevention and doing things right the first time. The company has laid down a set of principles to guide employees toward providing products, services, and information that consistently satisfy the needs of its customers:

> Treat anyone who uses your products, services or information, both within and outside of MPP, as your customer.
> Understand what your customer's needs are.
> Determine with your customer what requirements have to be met to satisfy those needs.
> Use every tool available to you to consistently meet those requirements.
> Change those requirements when your customer's needs change.

Everyone's job performance, including top management's, will in part be evaluated in terms of its contribution to Total Quality. Managers will often be asked to tolerate short-term business setbacks in time, work, and expense in return for long-term quality gains. Top management is expected to provide leadership by demonstrating support by example—setting personal quality goals, providing part-time trainers, scheduling progress reviews, participating on project teams with peers, and establishing annual quality improvement plans. Participation of all employees is essential.

Total Quality will rely on teamwork. The company believes that the best instances of Total Quality within MPP result when a cross section of people and functions join together to work toward a common goal. To encourage teamwork, Monsanto has established a Total Quality Commitment Group, which also serves as a resource and information center. Everyone can turn to this group for news about the experiences of those who have already put Total Quality to work. The group will also provide all MPP employees with Total Quality Orientation training, as well as offering specific training courses in such areas as annual quality improvement planning, supplier/customer needs analysis and quality measurement, quality costs/systems analysis, group dynamics/team methods, statistical process control, and design of experiments.

Quality Circles, which have become quite popular at a number of Monsanto plants, have been responsible for significant dollar savings. All of these plants, however, do not follow the traditional quality circle approach. Many prefer to mold the concept according to their own needs. At one location, for example, circle members have experimented with work teams in which each team member trains for all jobs in the team and then rotates among them. One of the initial benefits of this approach has been the elimination of a layer of management.

Monsanto has received substantial recognition for its dedication to Total Quality. Eastman Kodak selected MPP as a "Quality First" supplier, a designation reserved for its most valued suppliers. Another one of the company's customers, Vinyl Plastics, named MPP a preferred supplier. And Ford paid tribute by presenting three of MPP's plants with the Ford Q1 Preferred Quality Award. Obviously, the benefits to be derived from a commitment to quality are more than merely financial.

AMP INCORPORATED

In 1984, AMP Inc. of Harrisburg, Pennsylvania, a major manufacturer of electrical and electronic connection devices, sold $1.8 billion worth of parts worldwide and increased its exports of electrical connectors to over $130 million—an increase of about 30 percent from the previous year. Quite impressive, considering that many U.S. manufacturers had not fared nearly as well, because of intense competition abroad and the strength of the American dollar.

AMP's success is largely due to its continuing commitment to improved customer service. Growing demands in the market have presented the company with some great challenges. Today, their customers are requiring delivery within one day of scheduled dates of 95 percent of the lots shipped. Many customers have indicated that by the late 1980s they will need delivery of certain items within twenty-four hours in order to minimize their inventories. Additional demands for progressively higher levels of quality, service, and technological support have intensified the need for better customer service.

In 1985, AMP set out to improve component quality tenfold within five years. The company's quality improvement programs promote the process in house. Employees are heavily trained in statistical techniques and basic quality improvement concepts as they relate to all aspects of the company's business. There are currently 136 Quality Improvement Teams working cooperatively throughout the company. At the Selinsgrove plant, one team managed to save the company $88,000 by achieving a 400-percent reduction in the number of deviated lots over an eight-month period.

AMP employees also participate in a corrective-action program. When they encounter problems, they relate them to management, accompanied by corrective-action requests with suggestions for improvement. Thus far, over 5,000 corrective-action requests have been submitted, and over 75 percent of them have been implemented.

Digital Equipment is one firm that has recognized the company's efforts to deliver quality components on time. In March of 1985, AMP met its one-day performance goal with a 92-percent delivery rate to DEC's Albuquerque plant—a substantial improvement over January's 27-percent and February's 59-percent on-time shipping rate. DEC sent AMP employees a congratulatory letter, and the company's Signal Components Division was honored with two plaques. DEC named the division a valued participating supplier in their "Just In Time/Total Quality Control" process. The division was also named a participating Ship-To-Stock supplier for 1985 by DEC's plant in Colorado Springs.

Just as their customers have placed increasing demands on them, so too has AMP placed increasing demands on its own suppliers. Long-term relationships with fewer suppliers, based on mutual trust, confidence, and good communications, are becoming the modus operandi. Suppliers are expected to strive continuously to provide products that conform 100 percent to requirements. Should suppliers be unable to make products to specifications, they are obligated to inform AMP and work jointly with AMP's engineers to resolve whatever problems they may have. Suppliers' abilities to conform to quality and delivery requirements are evaluated and related back to them in the form of a "Supplier Quality and Delivery Performance Report." Suppliers must study these reports and take any corrective action needed to maintain performance levels. AMP is nearing the point where it will require all of its suppliers to implement statistical process control.

Suppliers are also expected to cut their production costs. AMP believes this can be done by working closely with them to develop alternate lower cost materials, new and improved processes, and new types of equipment. AMP has made several other provisions for cutting costs. These include longer commitments to the supplier through blanket orders, systems contracts, and annual contracts, increased standardization of materials, redesign and value analysis, and investments in tooling or automation at the suppliers' location.

"On-time delivery," AMP's version of just-in-time purchasing, has been established through the company's materials-planning management system. The company has set some exacting requirements for delivery performance: plus/minus five days to purchase-order schedule on 90 percent of lots shipped in 1986, leading toward plus/minus one day to purchase order schedule on 95 percent of lots shipped in 1988. To help the supplier meet these requirements, AMP will be responsible for:

1. Providing improved forecasting capabilities to deliver reliable forecasts in the appropriate format. Forecasters that have access to a continuous flow of updated information will minimize the risks for all parties,

2. Reducing the number of schedule changes,
3. Allowing for annual contracts,
4. Providing for fewer orders and change orders to manage, and
5. Allowing for longer raw-material commitments.

Purchases will be made through an on-line information system that will permit electronic transfers of information, direct access to the supplier computer for order entry and inquiry, and open order reports to help manage supplier capacity.

AMP expects its suppliers to accept several responsibilities as well in order to meet the goal of on-time delivery. They must agree to:

1. Accept no orders with schedules that can't be met,
2. Insist on formal change notices on schedules, hot lists, and the like that will adversely affect orders on the books,
3. Put material on AMP's dock on the scheduled date,
4. Provide advance notification to AMP if delivery is going to change,
5. Maintain adequate tooling, spare parts, and production equipment, and
6. Provide for flexibility in schedule changes and emergency needs.

AMP's long-range goal is to become the ultimate supplier. According to Walter Raab, chairman and chief executive, and Harold McInnes, AMP's president, "that means having a policy of early involvement (working closely with customers at the design stage in developing new products), clearly understanding the specific requirements of the customer, designing products that precisely meet those requirements, efficiently producing products exactly conforming to those requirements and doing so at competitive prices." McInnes claims that communication with the customer is a must. "All too frequently," he says, "the basic specification for a product is inadequate, or incomplete in terms of describing the full set of true needs for the product, while purchaser and supplier alike are comforted by page after page of detailed documentation. Suppliers need to apply their specialized expertise to help customers determine their true, long-term requirements."[8]

Reducing costs, management believes, is essential to remain competitive, and this is most effectively done by providing employees with an environment that will encourage and enable them to do their jobs in the best way possible. The content of most jobs has been changing at a very rapid pace due to factory and office automation, computer integration, and electronic communication. As McInnes puts it:

> This changing job content is combined with a far different work force—one made up of workers who expect more and more to be treated as individuals, to be kept informed, to participate, and to contribute. We are entering the age of the discretionary worker. Success of quality improvement will obviously rest on how well management has won over the hearts and minds of employees and received their commitments to excellence.[9]

NOTES

1. "Excellence in Ohio: We've Only Scratched the Surface,": *Ohio Business*, February 1985.
2. Remarks made at a luncheon in New York City, January 17, 1985.
3. Roger B. Smith, "A Working Partnership for Managing Change" (Speech given to the Management Research Center as part of the Baird/Manegold Lecture Series, The University of Wisconsin-Milwaukee, October 31, 1984).
4. Roger B. Smith, (Remarks at the Groundbreaking Ceremony UAM/GM Human Resource Center, Auburn Hills, Michigan, May 9, 1985).
5. F. James McDonald, "Entrepreneurship in a 'Mature Industry'" (Speech given to the fifth Conference of the U.S.-Japan Automotive Industry, Ann Arbor, Michigan, March 5, 1985).
6. Russell Mitchell, "How Ford Hit the Bull's-Eye with Taurus,": *Business Week*, June 30, 1986, 70.
7. Ibid.
8. "Successful Changes Anticipated Through Teamwork," *Quality Connection* no. 8, July 1985, 1.
9. Ibid.

10 THE FUTURE

Industrial effectiveness and productivity are undergoing revolutionary changes due to: (1) intense international competition generated by rapidly increasing manufacturing capabilities; (2) changes in union-management relationships; (3) the alteration of conventional organizational structures and ownership patterns; and (4) major advances in manufacturing technologies.

This modern industrial revolution has been accelerated by the emergence of the Japanese industrial juggernaut. Over the past two decades, a tidal wave of Japanese products has reached our shores, ranging from automobiles to watches to personal computers, all distinguished by their quality, innovativeness, and price. Today we are also seeing a flow of consumer and industrial goods from South Korea, Taiwan, Singapore, and other emerging industrial nations. To compensate for the loss of some foreign markets, Japan is branching out with high technology products such as supercomputers and lasers, as well as worldwide financial services. The effects of this new influx will be felt far into the future both in the United States and Europe.

To maintain its place under the industrial sun, the United States has begun to fight back. President Reagan, realizing the problems the country was facing, signed legislation on October 25, 1982, calling for a White House Conference on Productivity to develop recommendations for stimulating productivity growth in the United States. A series of preparatory conferences was held prior to the final White House Conference. One of the more interesting of these was conducted over a four-month period in 1983 at the American Productivity Center in Houston, Texas.[1] The 175 senior-level leaders from business, labor, academia, and government present at the conference arrived at this consensus:

1. Management at all levels should be less authoritarian and more interactive.

2. Organized labor should accept greater responsibility for the competitiveness of its employing firms.

3. Government is responsible for moderating the human impact of the competitive process.

4. Private cooperations and schools should work to raise quality awareness through campaigns to spread concepts of quality and national awards for contributions to improved quality.

5. Reward systems for productivity improvement should be initiated, including sharing business information with employees, introducing participative work practices, paying for performance, and designing better measurement of productivity.

6. Strong programs of education and training should be established to enhance management skills in the development and utilization of new technology.

7. Government procurement practices should be changed to include provisions for sharing increases in risk and reductions in cost due to implementation of new technology.

The summation conference was held in Washington, D.C., on September 21–23, 1983, chaired by L. William Seidman and William Simon.[2] The findings and recommendations of the preparatory conferences were presented and discussed before approximately 1000 attendees, and suggestions for future action were sought. Listed below are some of the major policy recommendations produced by the conference:

A. Government Actions

1. Increase public recognition and acceptance of improving productivity growth as a national goal and as the means to raise our standard of living through:

a. consistently evaluating regulations and laws in terms of effects on productivity;

b. creating a National Medal for Productivity and Quality Achievement; and

c. emphasizing better techniques to measure productivity.

2. Maintain a stable noninflationary economy and reduce the government's consumption of national resources.

3. Develop a specific plan for fundamental tax reform, using improving productivity as a standard to evaluate proposals.

4. Change or repeal laws that impede productivity growth, by means of:

a. setting performance standards in environmental regulation;

b. incorporating cost-benefit analyses and market-based incentives into health and safety regulation;

c. protecting patents against unfair use by other countries, especially in the areas of computer software and microchip technology;

d. making joint ventures, including joint R&D ventures, a more effective way to meet world competition;

e. removing constraints on competition in energy, communications, transportation, and financial-services industries.

B. Private-Sector Actions

1. Focus more attention on improving technology, quality, and information resources.

2. Employ creative, innovative work practices to take full advantage of the knowledge and talents of employees.

3. Establish productivity measures and improvement goals, especially for information and service workers.

4. Promote labor-management cooperation in considering workplace problems such as plant closings, training, restrictive practices, and employment security.

It should be obvious to the reader that the conferences did forge most of the nuts, bolts, and components basic to the American transitional model. It is equally obvious that, since the report was issued in late 1983, not much has occurred. Few of the suggestions made by some of our leading businessmen, government officials, and academics have become national policy—if there is such a thing as a national policy regarding business. Our industrial competitiveness and productivity are still major concerns. These problems will radically affect our overall economic and social well-being unless they are dealt with in the near future.

As part of the solution, we have developed what we believe to be a useful structural tool. Our American transitional model is predicated on the willingness of American companies to operate on a long-term basis. We tend to favor year-to-year operating results over long-range accomplishments with the potential for positive future payoffs. Indeed, many companies find it difficult to obtain long-term backing because our financial system favors short-term, high-return investments. This inability to finance long-term projects helps prevent us from competing in many world markets. Roger Brown and Melissa Altman put it succinctly:

> The capital markets' short-term bias, which has developed over the past decade, robs industry of the capital it needs to move new technologies out of the lab and into the market. Investors' time horizons are now out of step with the incubation periods of critical technologies.[3]

To compound matters, individual results—and hence rewards—are based on the short or proximate term, which discourages executives from actively engaging in true long-range planning. American managers have a difficult time surviving when their companies' earnings are low or static for even a few years. They correctly perceive that their careers are far more dependent on the short run than on the promise of higher earnings in the future. They know it is very difficult to explain to most stockholders that current profits and dividends are not as important as future earnings and eventual increased dividends. To reach that desired future, a firm must increase its market share, seek entrance into new markets, and invest in research and development. All these activities must be financed with current profits or loans, which will result in lower current earnings and probably lower stock prices. Management must be prepared to face stockholder dissatisfaction. The prospect is painful, but American firms will have to accept the possibility if they are to achieve their goals.

The model also address the concept of quality. There can be no doubt that if commitment to quality is to permeate an organization, it must begin at the top. Executive management must constantly stress its dedication to continual quality improvement, never giving the impression that quality is a passing fad. It must strive through its actions and educational programs to involve all its employees and suppliers in quality consciousness. In addition, everyone must be made to realize that the pursuit of quality must be unremitting if we are to survive in this competitive world. The quality process is not limited to manufacturing; it is equally important in the service and administrative functions of the organization. And the ultimate proof of the pudding will be that the customer is satisfied with the taste.

It is possible for us to overcome the industrial and economic problems we are now facing. All of our firms, not just a select few, must realize that the time for change is now. We must be willing to subjugate our pride and egos, to accept these new ideas, technologies, processes, and methodologies that make such good economic sense and blend them with the best we have to offer. Our competitive future will depend on how well American industry can develop, adapt, and apply advanced product and process technologies. To complement these technological advances, we need to revise our management practices and concepts, to develop new and modern organizational structures, and to build a constructive relationship, verging on a form of partnership, between labor and management. We must be able to provide world-class competitive products and services in order to achieve a prosperous future.

The use of the transitional model presented here could be a major first step along the pathway to American industrial and economic security.

NOTES

1. Computer Conferences on Productivity, *A Final Report for the White House Conference on Productivity* (Houston: American Productivity Center, 1983).
2. White House Conference on Productivity, *Productivity Growth: A Better Life for America* (Washington, D.C.: U.S. Government Printing Office, 1984).
3. Roger Brown and Melissa Altman, "Ridding Wall Street of a Short-Term Bias," *New York Times*, Sunday, June 1, 1986, Business Section, p. 3.

APPENDIX

"December 14, 1985

"Dear Sir:

"We, Dr. Harris Jack Shapiro, Director of the Center of Management, and Teresa Cosenza, Doctoral Student in Management Planning Systems, of Baruch College, The City University of New York, are currently engaged in researching materials for our forthcoming book concerning the applicability of Japanese management techniques in American industry.

"We are wondering if you could possibly accommodate us in our research by providing information regarding the use of Japanese techniques in your organization such as organizing employee teams, involving the employee in the decision-making process, adopting a paternalistic attitude toward the employee (e.g., offering job security and providing recreational and cultural activities for the employee), implementing a company-wide system of quality control, training employees as generalists rather than specialists, and utilizing the just-in-time system of inventory control. If you have implemented any Japanese techniques, we are very interested in learning how you were able to implement them and how you overcame any problems you may have had by implementing techniques which may have run counter to both the American worker's traditional perception of his or her position in the corporation and the American supplier's traditional perception of its relationship with the buying firm. In addition, if you feel that Japanese techniques would not fare well in your organization, we are also interested the reasons this may be so.

"If you would be so kind to provide us with this and any other information related to the use of Japanese techniques in your organization, and should you further permit us to publish such information, we would be most grateful. Thanking you for your attention, we remain

"Sincerely yours,"

HERSHEY FOODS

Letter from L. Philip Rothermel, director of productivity improvement, Hershey Foods Corporation, Hershey, Pennsylvania, December 16, 1985.

" . . . Hershey Foods Corporation employs all the "Japanese" techniques cited in your letter with the exception of JIT inventory control. The reason for putting "Japanese" in quotes is twofold.

"First, many of the methods or systems mentioned have been in practice at Hershey for many years, certainly before the Japanese became internationally recognized as management innovators. Hershey Chocolate Company, Friendly Ice Cream Corporation, and the individual companies that make up the Hershey Pasta Group have utilized paternalistic management styles from their beginnings. Mr. Hershey, in particular, had established a model community providing not only jobs but education and recreation for the employees since the early 1900s.

"I personally, as well as several of my colleagues, have had the opportunity of a generalist rather than a specialist background beginning in the late 1960s. While not all employees are lucky enough to receive this type of training, many are given the opportunity provided they are open enough to accept.

"Task teams, likewise, have been used since the late 60s to solve problems and the corporate food and safety and quality programs emphasize employee involvement in many aspects of the development and operation.

"You are probably aware that many of the "Japanese" techniques were developed by Americans. As in other areas, the Japanese improved on the methods provided by outsiders.

"The second reason for the quotes is that depending on the technique it may be impossible to implement in an American company. Having lived and worked in the Orient for the last five years, I know (not necessarily understand) the vast differences between people in the Orient and the Western World. While it may be possible that some of the more mechanical processes may be adapted to U.S. firms, in my opinion it is highly unlikely that a true Japanese system would work in any U.S. company with all U.S. workers. While many people have learned to enjoy oriental food, not all families are convinced that chop sticks are the best eating utensils. . . ."

OUTBOARD MARINE

Letter from Dennis W. Butt, director of manufacturing engineering, Outboard Marine Corporation, Waukegan, Illinois, February 18, 1986.

"The management techniques you refer to in your letter of 12/18/85 (attached) are not Japanese in origin. Organizing employee teams, involving employees in decisionmaking, implementing company-wide quality control systems, training employees as generalists, and Just-In-Time are all western in origin and should not, therefore, be referred to as Japanese techniques.

"I hasten to point out, as well, that Just-In-Time is not a 'system of inventory control.'

"Outboard Marine Corporation is adopting all of the above as our situation will allow, not because these techniques have an oriental aura, but because to the U.S. manufacturing professional, they are fundamental to the effectiveness of our profession.

"There has been much written on the subject you have choosen. We U.S. manufacturing professionals consider it all, without exception, to be lèse-majesté. It implies, at least, that we are inept or second-rate with respect to our counterparts in Japan, when the fact of the matter is that we are still, by far, the best manufacturing people in the world. Given the same set of circumstances we were given over the past couple of decades, no other nationality would have been able to save the profession.

"I suspect from what you have written that you assume that what others who have gone before you have written was well researched. You have that right indeed. Being able to believe what others tell us is the cement that holds society together. It is also the one tenuous nexus that allows our pool of knowledge to expand.

"I sincerely hope your book does American industry justice, and that it is constructive to all that read it. I hope, also, that it is of some value to U.S. manufacturing professionals. In order to be any of the above, however, you will have to be very carefully in choosing your assumptions. I know of nothing whatsoever that has written to date on the subject of Japanese Management Techniques that is akin to reality."

MITSUI (U.S.A.)

Letter from Kaneo Itoh, executive vice president, Mitsui & Co. (U.S.A.), Inc., New York, New York, January 14, 1986.

"In your letter of December 10 you inquired about the use of "Japanese" management techniques in our firm. (I am sure you are aware that Japan originally learned most of these techniques from the West.)

"As Mitsui & Co. is a general trading company, not a manufacturing company, some of the concerns you raised are not applicable. However, let me give you a quick sketch of management techniques at Mitsui that may be of interest.

"1. Mitsui USA (and our parent company in Japan), use the Ringi decisionmaking system that you have no doubt read about. Proposals for major new business, investments, large credit lines, and other important changes are usually initiated by middle management (often department heads). After preliminary discussion, a Ringi form is written and circulated to relevant department heads and executives, each of whom has a space to initial if they agree and to make comments. The Ringi works its way up to the president, who makes the final decision.

"2. Most of the Japanese who were sent here from Mitsui, Japan, were hired under the "Japanese" employment system that takes young people right out of universities and rotates them to various positions for training. Our American employees were hired on a more diverse basis, some for particular expertise and others for on-the-job training more like what is done in Japan.

"3. The company does have some recreational and cultural activities, but perhaps no more than many U.S. firms have. For example, there is a company golf tournament, and some cultural/educational courses (Ikebana flower arranging, Japanese language) offered.

"4. Regarding job security, many of our American employees do stay and make a career at Mitsui, each year-end the company gives out a number of awards for 10, 15, and 20-year service, and if a department no longer needs a staff member, an effort is often made to place him or her in another department. But there is no formalized commitment to 'lifetime employment.' . . . ."

ENPLAS (U.S.A.)

Letter from Ken Esaki, vice president, Enplas (U.S.A.) Inc., Smyrna, Georgia, January 23, 1986.

"Thank you for asking Enplas (U.S.A.) Inc. to participate in your research project. While we have many Japanese management techniques in the organization, many are not so different from those used by American companies. I will try to respond to your letter by topic.

"1. Employee teams—If by employee teams you mean quality circles, the answer is no. However, we do make a significant effort to have people involved at all levels in the operations of the company. We have a J.I.C. (Job Improvement Committee) which meets monthly to discuss way to make the work environment more pleasant and safer. The J.I.C. committee is made up of the Policies and Benefits committee, the Safety and Housekeeping committee, and the Suggestion committee.

"These committees make recommendations and requests of management. The final decision to make changes resides with management.

"2. Paternalistic Attitude toward employees. No more than an American company and less paternalistic than large American firms. Job security is a function of our ability to obtain orders for our products and fill those orders to the satisfaction of our customers. We do have something called Enplas Clubs. Enplas Clubs are funded jointly by the company and the employees. Enplas Clubs provide for the recreation of the employees.

"3. Quality Control—We are in business today because of our ability to produce a consistently high-quality product. Everyone in the company is aware that quality is of paramount importance.

"4. Our people tend to be specialists instead of generalists.

"5. We do use just-in-time inventory system where possible."

INDEX

ABOUT THE AUTHORS

Harris Jack Shapiro is a professor of management and director of the Center for Management at Bernard M. Baruch College of the City University of New York. He was previously chairman of the Department of Management. Before joining the university, he founded, and served as president and chief executive officer of, Ogden Technology Laboratories, Inc., a subsidiary of the Ogden Corporation that specializes in aerospace research, development, and testing. Dr. Shapiro has sat on several corporate boards of directors and does consulting and research in the field of strategic management. He is a professional engineer, holding a B.M.E. cum laude from City College, the City University of New York; an M.S. in management engineering from Long Island University; an M.B.A. from Baruch College; and a Ph.D. with distinction from the Graduate Center of the City University of New York. He has published two books and many articles in journals such as *Management Science, Decision Science*, the *Academy of Management Journal*, the *Academy of Management Review*, and *Long Range Planning.*

Teresa Cosenza is an instructor of statistics at Hofstra University's School of Business. She holds a B.A. in foreign languages from Adelphi University and an M.B.A. from Hofstra University.